Glastonbury, the Templars and the Sovran Cloth

✝

A new Perspective on the Grail Legends

T0346694

GLASTONBURY, THE TEMPLARS AND THE SOVRAN CLOTH

✛

NEW PERSPECTIVE ON THE GRAIL LEGENDS

JULIET FAITH

The
History
Press

First published 2012
Reprinted 2013

The History Press
The Mill, Brimscombe Port
Stroud, Gloucestershire, GL5 2QG
www.thehistorypress.co.uk

British Library Cataloguing in Publication Data.
A catalogue record for this book is available from the British Library.

ISBN 978 0 7524 7025 2

Typesetting and origination by The History Press
Printed in Great Britain

CONTENTS

ACKNOWLEDGEMENTS

Many of those who helped with the research of my previous book, *The Knights Templar in Somerset*, have again enthusiastically helped and supported me with the material for this book.

My special thanks go to retired NASA scientist and Shroud scholar Ed Prior, who I met when he visited England in 2010 to lecture about Joseph of Arimathea and the Turin Shroud. I did not feel that I had researched Joseph of Arimathea fully enough to deal at length with the vexed question, 'Did Joseph bring Christianity to England?' Therefore, Ed has written a special 'paper' to be included in this book on my behalf (*see* Appendix). Ed has been researching Joseph of Arimathea for many years, and is working on his own book about early Christianity. I am greatly honoured that he has taken the time and trouble to write for this book; for this I owe him a debt of gratitude.

Special thanks once again to Shroud researcher and international author Rex Morgan, with whom I have been 'comparing notes' on the activities of the Knights Templar in England. Rex and I met last year on his visit to this country, and I am most grateful that he has made his early research available to me. One chapter of this book includes the fascinating research that he and his team conducted in the 1980s concerning the Templecombe Panel.

Thank you once again to Barbara Birchwood Harper and Daniel Agee of the Looe Old Cornwall Society, who gave me some enlightening information on the connections between Looe Island and Glastonbury Abbey. Daniel has written several very interesting essays on the Cornwall/Glastonbury connection.

Thank you also to Paul Ashdown, whose own research work in some ways touches on my own, and has provided some interesting insights.

Many thanks to my friend and neighbour Becky, for her delightful illustrations. Also to Ken Macfarlane for freely giving his time to take photographs for the book, not to forget Elizabeth Blaymires, who popped through my letterbox an old folk poem recited to her by her grandmother when she was a child in 1948, entitled 'The Son of Man on Mendip'.

Others who have assisted either directly or indirectly are: Kevin Spears, Wells Cathedral Librarian; Tom Bree; Susan Hannis; Clive Wilkins;

Dr Simon Johnson; Dr Harvey Thompson; the staff at Glastonbury Abbey; the staff at Winchester Cathedral, and the Hospital of St Cross; the staff at Looe Museum and Glastonbury Abbey.

Also, my thanks to all those who have offered time and support in many other ways during the writing of this book.

Last but not least my special thanks to Fi Bannister, who has walked the sacred places with me, and encouraged and supported me in many ways over the past few years; Harvey Thompson, who is 'on the path'; and my sons Tristan and Tobias, who have shared all the highs and lows that my research entails!

INTRODUCTION

Since time immemorial, Glastonbury has acted as a magnet for pilgrims, saints, sinners and tourists alike. It appears that many are drawn to the place for some reason unknown to themselves. Many, if not most, are seeking something, but what? Perhaps they seek to find or understand the elusive Grail?

Here at Glastonbury we find stories that tell of Joseph of Arimathea visiting Somerset as a tin merchant, accompanied by the boy Jesus; legends of King Arthur; whispers of a faery realm within the Tor; and the ruins of what was arguably once the greatest abbey in England. There are tantalising tales of the cup of the Last Supper, hidden in the Chalice Well, and whispers of fragments of the shroud of Christ once venerated at a Perilis Chapel.

In researching this book, I wanted to explore whether there was any truth behind these tales: were they mere fabrication, or could it be that once, long ago, someone or something of unique and sacred importance arrived in England and found its way to Somerset?

Since writing my previous book, *The Knights Templar in Somerset*, I found I was certainly not alone in my beliefs – others had been thinking in a similar way, and several have contacted me to tell me about their own research and ideas. As a consequence of this, I have been fortunate enough to meet and spend time with both Shroud scholar and international author Rex Morgan, and Ed Prior, retired NASA scientist and Shroud scholar. Rex has shared his research on the Templecombe Panel

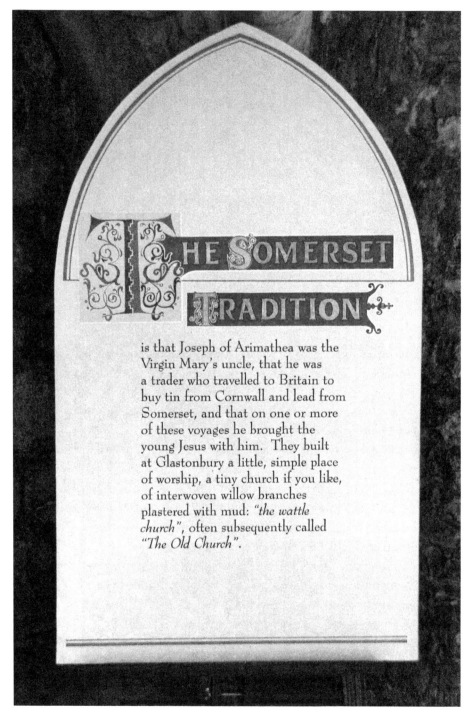

THE SOMERSET TRADITION

is that Joseph of Arimathea was the Virgin Mary's uncle, that he was a trader who travelled to Britain to buy tin from Cornwall and lead from Somerset, and that on one or more of these voyages he brought the young Jesus with him. They built at Glastonbury a little, simple place of worship, a tiny church if you like, of interwoven willow branches plastered with mud: *"the wattle church"*, often subsequently called *"The Old Church"*.

'The Somerset Tradition', Glastonbury Abbey. (Courtesy of Ken Macfarlane)

with me, while Ed has imparted his knowledge of Joseph of Arimathea in a special 'appendix' section of the book.

Their ideas reinforced my own conviction that there could indeed be a connection between the mysterious legends of the Holy Grail and the relic known as the Holy Shroud of Turin, and these grail legends led to the heart of my home county, Somerset, and most especially to Glastonbury.

Perhaps the legends and folk memories which have been passed down to us through the ages are more than just stories; within them we may find an ancient memory of a much greater, more mysterious and inspirational truth …

Juliet Faith, 2012

'THE SON OF MAN ON MENDIP'

(An Old Somerset Poem)

The Son of Man on Mendip
He walked among the fern
Against the blackness of the down
He saw the heather turn.
The Son of Man on Mendip
Gazed down the glistening tide
Beyond the sprinkled Islands
Where the grey lagoons spread wide.

For Joseph was a tinman
Who sailed the Western sea
And brought his young companion
Across to Eggarley.
Where amid the golden orchards
Whose scent the silence thrills
The Lamb of God in beauty trod
Our Avalonian hills.

The Son of Man on Mendip
He gave the folk no sign,
But talked and walked with such as worked
The led and coalmine.
He knew the old Nine Barrows,
The swallets and the droves,
As well as, on far southern slopes,
He knew the orange groves.

As summer passed to autumn,
He marked the changing days.
The blood red wicken berries
In Ebbor Gorge ablaze.
The crocus in the meadows,
The gold upon the wheat,
And snow-white bog cotton
Bent to those gentle feet.

The Son of Man on Mendip
He breathed the common air
And so folk tell by word of mouth,
He played at Priddy Fair.
For Joseph was a tinman
Who dealt in dyes and ores.
Trading from torrid Nazareth
To Somerset's green shores.

On Easter morning
When the clouds be rolled away,
And climbing Maesbury beacon
The young sun brings the day,
They that be simple hearted
That nothing ill have done,
A wondrous sign may witness
The Lamb against the sun.

THE SHROUD OF TURIN –
THE TRUE BURIAL
SHROUD OF CHRIST?

Much of this book is concerned with a presumed burial linen or shroud of Jesus, and the importance that it had historically, and may still have for us today. I therefore decided that it was prudent to give a short synopsis of the only real contender for the title the 'true burial Shroud of Jesus'; that is the cloth known today as the Shroud of Turin.

Sceptics delight in commenting that there were once many presumed 'Shrouds of Christ'. Certainly during the sixteenth and seventeenth centuries there were known to be about fifty contenders for the shroud, some examples of which still survive to this day, such as the one displayed in the church of Notre Dame de Chambery, which is a watercolour on fabric[i].

The Lier Shroud, commissioned by a member of the Savoy family,[ii] is believed to have been be painted by Durer in 1516. As a historical record it is of great interest, but is clearly the work of an artist.

However, what these 'shrouds' do tell us, from strange details on each, is that there were attempts to copy an original cloth with a figure imprinted upon it, but with very limited success.

The idea that the shroud which Joseph of Arimathea provided to wrap the body of Jesus in, after his crucifixion 2,000 years ago, could survive to this day appears to be an incredible and unlikely idea. However, in Turin Cathedral there is an ancient piece of linen which may be that very cloth.

The Shroud of Turin is a 14-feet long piece of linen bearing on it the shadowy imprint – both front and back – of a bearded, crucified man. The figure bears witness to the biblical accounts of Jesus's Passion and crucifixion. We know that the Shroud of Turin is not a drawing, not a painting, and not a photograph, but to date we do not know with certainty how it was made.

This subtle, sepia-coloured image shows a man who has been beaten, scourged, speared in the side and crucified. The cloth contains bloodstains – real human blood – and, horrifyingly, traces of human muscle tissue[iii] from the appalling wounds he sustained. The blood flow from the wound in the side indicates a mixture of blood and fluid. Doctors agree that the fluid is plasma, caused either by a puncture wound to the heart or from a build up of fluids in the chest cavity caused by the trauma of flogging, and are entirely consistent with medical reality.[iv]

The shroud also contains pollens from the Middle East and Europe, burn marks, limestone from Jerusalem, water stains and traces of anointing spices. Each of these elements tell their own story; they indicate that the shroud traveled from place to place, collecting evidence along the way of where it was housed or displayed during its long history.

Dr Max Frei, a Swiss botanist and criminologist, took samples from the surface of the Shroud of Turin in 1976. His findings revealed pollens from many different species of plants, which provide evidence that the shroud had been present in the Holy Land, Europe and Turkey. His findings confirmed Ian Wilson's theories as to where the Shroud had historically been located at different points in history. In 1981, Frei had identified further pollens, fifty-seven varieties in total. These confirm that the shroud had been present in France and Italy, near the Dead Sea, Palestine, Anatolia and Constantinople, to name but a few. Some of these pollens were from plants which are now extinct.[v]

Very interestingly, around the head area of the man on the shroud was found a cluster of pollens from the thorn plant *Gundelia Tourifortii*, which grows in the vicinity of Jerusalem. This finding provides evidence for the 'crown of thorns', or more likely a crude cap of thorns, which the Bible tells us was placed on Jesus's head to mock him. In fact, all the wounds found on the body of the man in the shroud, concur precisely with the Gospel descriptions of Jesus's Passion and crucifixion.

The infamous carbon-14 dating of 1988, which declared the Shroud of Turin to be of medieval origin and therefore a fake, has almost unanimously been discredited.

It appears that the laboratory samples for the testing were taken from a corner of the shroud, where documentary evidence shows us that it was held up for display over the centuries. Not only would this area have been contaminated, but recent findings presented by sindonologists Joe Marino and the late Sue Benford, confirmed by research from Scientist Raymond Rogers, show the sample taken for the carbon-14 dating to be a medieval re-weave.

But the mystery still remains, how was the image formed? Despite years of exhaustive study (the Shroud of Turin is the most studied artifact on the planet) and many different theories being put forward, science still cannot conclusively tell us how it came to be.

The image is a photographic negative, and was only clearly revealed to us with the advent of photography. In 1898, an Italian photographer, Secondo Pia, photographed it for the first time and was astonished to find that his negative plate showed an incredibly life-like image – a far cry from the ghostly negative that can be seen on the cloth. Moving forward in time, the next astonishing event occurred as Scientist Dr John Jackson, of the US Air force Academy, placed a picture of the image into a VP-8 image analyzer, and incredibly the image on the shroud leapt into 3D relief. This was a unique occurrence; amazingly, it appears that the shroud is somehow encoded with 3D information!

The latest scientific view, and one that caught the newspaper headlines recently, is that the image on the Shroud was formed by a sudden, very short burst of ultraviolet radiation[vi], though not radiation as we understand it. Incredibly, this burst of radiant light was only enough to mark the surface fibrils of the cloth.

Dr John Jackson, a member of the 1978 Shroud of Turin Research Project (STURP)[vii] team, put forward the hypothesis some years ago that light, or radiation, had formed the image on the cloth. Most of STURP's findings have now been published in scientific journals.

Recent research carried out by a British doctor, Andrew Silverman, has produced some awe-inspiring and plausible possibilities. Dr Silverman's research, based upon quantum theory, suggests that matter, space and time are interrelated, with mind being the key mover in reality. He suggests that matter, space and time became separated at the time of the 'Big Bang'. Mind, he hypothesizes, is eternal, with no beginning and no end. The thought here is that Jesus, as a uniquely enlightened being, was able to somehow exert mind over matter, and, after his death, was able to leave an imprint on the shroud to illustrate to us that we are all capable of potentially greater actions than we

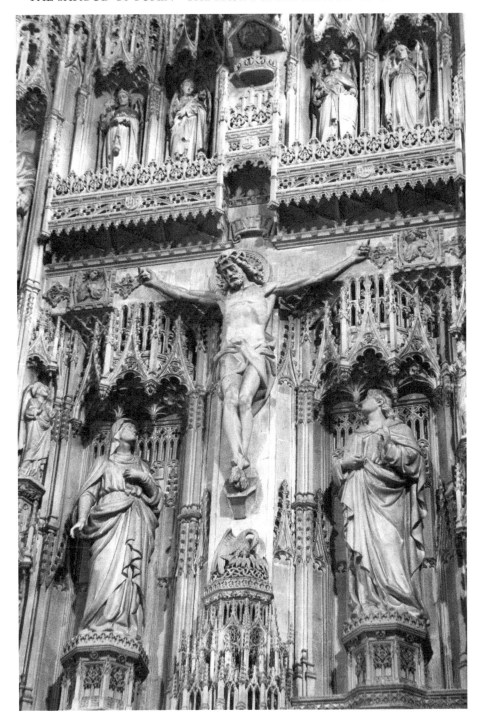

The Crucifixion; Reredos, Winchester Cathedral. (Courtesy of Ken Macfarlane)

believe. On several occasions in the Gospels, Jesus is recorded as becoming radiant in some way. Silverman sites the theories of Erwin Schrodinger, one of the founders of quantum theory.[viii]

Dr Silverman suggests that the blood from the corpse soaked into the shroud *before* the image was formed, that is whilst Jesus's body lay on a stone slab in the tomb. He believes that the body was upright, suspended in the air, when radiant light was somehow projected onto the cloth and the image formed on the shroud:

> On the Shroud of Turin, there is evidence that the dead body of a man who had suffered torture and crucifixion arose into a vertical position before momentarily shining brighter than the sun. The implications of this are considered for our understanding of space, time, matter and gravity. Also the implications are considered for our understanding of the nature of humanity and sentient awareness in general. It is considered whether these two lines of enquiry might one day lead to a unified understanding of the nature of existence itself.[ix]

ENDNOTES

i   Wilson I., *Shroud*. p.11/12 (Bantam, 2010)
ii   Morgan, R. (Ed.), *Shroud News*, No.113 (April 1999)
iii Nitowski, Dr E., 'The Body of Christ', *Shroud News*, No.100 (February 1997)
iv   The Shroud of Turin has been studied by various medical men, amongst whom were surgeon Dr Pierre Barbet; Dr David Willis; Dr Robert Bucklin, and Dr Antony Sava. All agree that the wounds and blood flows of the man in the shroud are medically correct. (*See* Ian Wilson, *The Shroud* (2010) and *The Blood and the Shroud* (1998). Frale, B. *The Templars and the Shroud of Christ*)
v   Morgan, R., *Shroud Guide* (The Runciman Press, 1983)
vi   Pi di Lazarro, (Ed.), *Journal of Imaging Science and Technology*, (July/August 2010)
vii Shroud of Turin Research Project. In 1978, a team of research scientists were granted round-the-clock access to the Shroud of Turin in an attempt to try and discover how the image had been formed. The team, comprising of some of the worlds finest scientific minds, was led by Dr John Jackson
viii Silverman, Dr Andrew, *The Light that Shone in the Darkness*, www.lightoftheshroud.com
ix   *Ibid.*

1

THE ARRIVAL OF CHRISTIANITY IN SOUTH-WEST BRITAIN

Christianity in these lands was not Roman but Celtic, and to the Celtic Christians the Pope was but one bishop among many. Devout men and women carried the light of faith to the wild tribes of the north and west, but they looked to holy Ireland, not to Rome, for their inspiration.[i]

Situated on Looe Island and opposite on the mainland at Hannafore, near Looe in Cornwall, are two ancient chapels. The area was originally known by its Celtic name Lammana. Although the documented history of the chapels at Lammana date back to 1144, archaeological and mythological evidence is suggestive of a much earlier settlement, one that stretched back in time not only to early Christian settlers in Britain, but seemingly long before then.

On arrival in Britain in AD 597, St Augustine probably found a country that was largely pagan, but in the 'western confines of Britain', he found 'the first neophites of Catholic law'.[ii]

Records confirm that in 1144, Lammana was included in a list of possessions that were confirmed to Glastonbury by Lucius II, and in 1203 a charter of Hasculf de Soligny, Lord of Portlooe, states that the lands at Lammana – including Looe Island – had been gifted to Glastonbury Abbey by his ancestors *ab antique* (from ancient times), although there is no mention of Lammana in the Domesday Charter. At this period in history, the properties of Lammana consisted of two chapels and a monks' house.[iii]

The early Celtic settlement. (Illustration by Rebecca Gryspeerdt)

It would certainly appear that during the time that Henry de Blois was Abbot of Glastonbury, Lammana was regarded as a place of extreme importance. It was probably during this time that the Norman chancels were added to the existing chapels both on the mainland and on the island. Why exactly Glastonbury was so interested in Lammana is not known exactly, but it is surely most likely connected to the early Celtic origins of the place. Reverend Picken comments:

> It is difficult to believe that the great Somersetshire abbey (Glastonbury) would have undertaken the maintenance of so small, remote and inconvenient a property as Lammana in Cornwall unless it was already the focus of a local cult of some distinction and that would predicate the presence of a chapel there. [iv]

Ruins of the Great Abbey, Glastonbury. (Courtesy of Ken Macfarlane)

The ruins of the nave at Glastonbury Abbey. (Courtesy of Ken Macfarlane)

Daniel Agee, who has made careful studies of the history of Lamanna,[v] suggests that in the Middle Ages, Glastonbury claimed the foundation story of Lammana and the associations with Joseph of Arimathea as its own, as a way to further boost the status and income of Glastonbury Abbey. Archaeologist C.K. Croft Andrew suggests that although Lammana probably had the earlier foundation, the Christian settlers may have moved 'up country' to Glastonbury, to establish another church there.

Daniel Agee notes that Dr Lynette Olsen observes that the Domesday Book only recorded 'secular manors in the Looe area.'[vi] It is probably because it was a religious establishment that Lammana was omitted from the Domesday Book.

C.K. Croft Andrew, who conducted some of the earliest excavations at the site, suggests the possibility that Lammana was *already* in the possession of the Abbey from as early as AD 722, when King Ina of Wessex gifted land in Cornwall to Glastonbury. The only land in Cornwall which was ever known to be in the possession of the Abbey was Lammana, so we can assume that this is most likely to be the land referred to in Ina's gift.

A charter of AD 725 states that 'all lands, places, and possessions of St Mary of Glastonbury be free quiet and undisturbed, from all royal taxes and works which are wont to be appointed.'[vii] It would appear then that Lammana was granted freedom from all forms of taxation.

Archaeological Surveys at Lammana

In 1935/6, Croft Andrew carried out the first extensive excavations at the ruins of Lammana. His findings were added to when, in 2009, Wessex Archaeology made another excavation of both the mainland and Looe Island sites.

It was discovered that Glastonbury Abbey had extended the two earlier chapels, which were both believed to be dedicated to St Michael. It also seems the Abbey added Norman chancels to the earlier naves that were already in existence.

In the chapel on the island the dig revealed a stone-lined reliquary in front of the altar. Under the wall of the chancel, but on the same level as the reliquary, a skeleton was discovered, indicating that Lammana was a place of pilgrimage *before* it was gifted to Glastonbury Abbey, as the chancel was Glastonbury work. Local lore speaks of certain relics of the Passion which were held at Lammana; and certainly at the time of the Dissolution, the King instructed that the chancel floor was to be dug up to find the treasure. The chapel was already in ruins at this time, so it is unlikely anything was found. It is thought that the 'relics' had been dispersed before the Dissolution.

A further discovery of two 'postholes' and a rock-cut feature suggested to the team that it was probable a wooden chapel pre-dated the stone chapel.

The two-storey 'monks' house' on the mainland site revealed a dwelling with thick walls and small windows, which contained two rooms for the monks, and a refectory for visitors. This also adds weight to the theory that Lammana was a pilgrimage site and an early Christian settlement. Records tell us that two Glastonbury monks originally inhabited the house.

On the island site there was evidence of an inhumation burial that had been found during earlier explorations in the 1800s; this burial revealed a rather statuesque skeleton (the discovery of this skeleton is documented in Thomas Bond's *Topographical and Historical Sketches of the Boroughs of East and West Looe* of 1823).

The archaeological team dug a further trench across an oval-shaped feature at the top of the island; they believed this feature to be suggestive of a prehistoric enclosure, probably re-used by later generations. Many early monasteries were constructed upon prehistoric sites. The enclosure would once have served as the boundary for the chapel; the same trench also revealed Roman finds – coins and pottery.

In the grounds of Island House, an excavation trench revealed what was believed to be a fallen standing stone. There is also a standing stone to the north of the island; both of these discoveries suggest prehistoric occupation.

The archaeological evidence points to the chapel on the island being the older of the two chapels.

A Modern Mystery

At the turn of the century, two men exploring Looe Island made a seemingly astonishing discovery. The headline in the *Cornish Times* of 15 September 1900 read, 'Remarkable Discoveries at Looe Island'.

It appears that two men, Mr R. Lawson from Inner Temple, London, and Mr F.A. Somers FSA, gained permission from Sir William Trelawney, the then owner of the island, to make some private explorations.

The two men made some seemingly incredible discoveries. It is claimed that they found adjoining caves, resembling Etruscan caves at Clusia in Italy. Further examination revealed a complex network of caves, some of which were built of brick, and although now submerged some 18 feet below the water, were presumably once above ground. It was speculated that these caves dated from about 800 BC. There was a further discovery of a cemetery and human remains, which were thought to belong to the time of the monastic settlement.

Despite the promise of the *Cornish Times* to publish a further article and precise details of the findings the following week, nothing ever appeared. Attempts were made to retrieve more information, but to no avail, and nothing more was heard of the discoveries or the men who made them.

Recently, Inner Temple was contacted to see whether they knew any more of Mr Lawson and his amazing findings. Although the archivist could confirm that he had worked at Inner Temple in the 1900s, she could find no reference to any exploration being made of Looe Island.

We are therefore left to wonder, would it be possible that these caves could have been used by the Phoenician's, who were believed to be very early traders to Cornwall, or were they smuggler's caves? Was the cemetery associated with Glastonbury Abbey, or was it from the time of the Celtic settlement on the island?

Until further excavations are made, underwater surveys are forthcoming, or the lost evidence re-appears, we can only speculate as to the validity of the claims.

Celtic Origins

It is almost certain that the first element of the Celtic name Lammana was originally the Cornish 'lan', which was a religious settlement of the Celtic type sometimes called monasteries, but more aptly described by Professor Charles Thomas as communal hermitages or perhaps eremitic communities.

Reverend Picken,
'Light on Lammana' Devon and Cornwall Notes and Queries 35

Scholars such as Lynette Olsen in her extensive study on the early monasteries of Cornwall[viii] have found that early Cornish churches and settlements indicate their Celtic origins with the prefix 'lan', which suggests a Celtic religious enclosure, which would have placed the chapel as central importance to their monastic group. These 'lans' would most probably have been important in pre-Christian times as the sacred place or sacred enclosure of the local tribe. The 'lan' prefix in Cornwall is the same as the Welsh 'llan'.

Another feature of these early Christian settlements is that they would frequently be named after their spiritual leader or founder. Daniel Agee's essay quotes Cornish historian and author W.H. Paynter, who suggests that the settlement at Lamanna was originally dedicated to St Manac (or

Manacus), hence the name lammana, meaning the community of, or founded by, St Manac. Others, including the Wessex Archaeology team, suggest that the name means simply 'monks' enclosure'. These early Christian settlements would originally have consisted of a single chapel or oratory (lan) surrounded by a small group of wattle huts, which would have provided the homes for a spiritual 'master' and his disciples.

Croft Andrew suggests that at Hannafore there was a cross on the beach at the location known as Cross Sands; and Agee notes that from the very springing of Christianity in Britain, believers would have gathered together in worship led by missionary monks, probably at the foot of stone preaching crosses. This could be the location where St Manacus first preached the gospel to the early Christians at Lamanna, long before the church was established there. A surprising number of ancient crosses can still be seen today in churchyards or near village centres, particularly in the Celtic regions of Britain – there are many fine examples of Celtic crosses to be seen in Wales, Scotland, Devon and Cornwall.

The ruins at Lammana have also been likened to two other Celtic Christian settlements in Cornwall: St Piran's oratory, and the oratory at St Gwithian's (now covered in sand).

This monastery at Lammana has similarities to the Celtic settlement at Beckery in Glastonbury. The area that contained the chapel and settlement are today known incorrectly as 'Bride's mound'.

The community at Beckery is thought to have been established by the Irish saint, Bridget, who was also the Abbess and founder of Kildare Abbey in Ireland in the fifth or sixth century. The cult of Bridget, however, goes back long before the establishment of her worship in the Celtic Church; in ancient times she was a fire deity, and goddess of the hearth and home.

What we can be certain of, however, is that by the Saxon and Middle Ages, Bridget was venerated at Glastonbury, and Beckery became a focal point for Irish pilgrims travelling to Glastonbury. The route to Glastonbury was taken by water; negotiating the marshy lands surrounding the island would have taken the travellers along the River Axe at Cheddar, through the Panborough Gap, past the ancient Glastonbury lake villages, and finally to Beckery, where excavations suggest there were ancient boat moorings.

In the High History of the Holy Grail, or Perlesvaus, legend tells that the original ancient chapel was dedicated to Mary Magdalene. If this is the case, then it was evidently re-named after Bridget settled at the location, and she – amongst other Irish saints such as Patrick and Indract – were venerated at Glastonbury.

Beckery Island. (Courtesy of Ken Macfarlane)

The first excavations at Beckery by John Morland took place in 1887; Morland discovered a chapel complex and priest's house. Like Lammana, the original chapel had been updated over time, starting as a shrine chapel, then being reconstructed in timber as an Anglo-Saxon monastery, and again in stone during the Norman period.[x]

Excavations undertaken in the ancient graveyard at Glastonbury Abbey (1951-1954) by Dr C.A. Ralegh Radford provided enough evidence for him to hypothesize that there had been a Celtic community present at Glastonbury before the Saxon conquest of Somerset in the seventh century. This is based on the finding of two large hypogea (underground burial chambers) that he believed could have housed the remains of St Indract and St Patrick. He also discovered evidence of the two 'pyramids' of which William of Malmesbury had spoken of in his chronicle.

Postholes in the cemetery were taken to be evidence of four wattled oratories, presumably of the same type believed to have been constructed at Lammana.

In the area between the two 'pyramids' (the suggested location of King Arthur's tomb), Radford found evidence of a 'large irregular hole, at the bottom of which could be seen the remnants of several very ancient slab-lined graves, one in a position of particular prominence'.

He further concluded that, 'A man such as Arthur, if resident in mid-Somerset in the sixth century, would probably have been buried at Glastonbury, and a warrior of his fame might be expected to be found buried alongside the mausoleum of the saint.'[xi]

Early Trade in the South-West

It is evident from the numerous archaeological discoveries that the South West of England was accessible to people travelling by sea from other parts of the world. Artefacts found in the water close to Looe Island are indicative of early trade in that area; these were the neck of an amphorae from the Mediterranean, and a tin and copper ingot. The estimated date of these finds is thought to be approximately 2,000 years old.

Not far away at Tintagel, a location associated with King Arthur and now belonging to English Heritage, fragments from hundreds of vessels were found at what is termed a 'high status' site. According to Lynette Olsen, 'Further excavation and study will probably show the occupation of Tintagel to have been more complex than has hitherto been supposed, as for example by the recovery of traces of wooden structures, it could prove to have been the site of an early monastery.'[xii] Certainly, archaeological finds here are suggestive of extensive overseas trade.

It would seem likely that the merchants were trading for Cornish tin; however, some scholars believe there was also trade in slaves, hunting dogs, skins, and gold and silver, in fact any moveable commodity that would be of value! It is now believed that over 1,500 years ago 'merchant ships brought pottery amphorae containing wine and olive oil, tableware, and glass drinking vessels from the shores of the Mediterranean and Aegean seas.'[xiii]

South Cadbury in Somerset is another site of great importance in the South West, both because of its Arthurian connections and its impressive archaeological yields, which also contain some Tintagel-type pottery.

Three different categories of pottery were discovered at South Cadbury, all of which provide evidence of trading from a very early period (c. AD 460/520). One particular style of pottery is described as 'rather fine red bowls, with wall-sided rims which are often decorated with rouletting. The bases have a shallow foot ring and sometimes bear stamped crosses on the interior. A source in the east Mediterranean is certain, but cannot be precisely located within an arc from Greece to Egypt.'[xiv]

There were also found varieties of amphorae for storage, and pottery thought to be from the Black Sea area of Romania; further examples are known to come from the Bordeaux area of France.

Leslie Alcock hypothesises that Cadbury Castle was re-occupied from approximately AD 470 by 'a community wealthy enough to take part in the trade which it demonstrates.'

Gateway – the entrance to Cadbury Castle. (Courtesy of Ken Macfarlane)

Ramparts at South Cadbury. (Courtesy of Ken Macfarlane)

Interestingly, pieces of similar Mediterranean ware were found at Glastonbury Tor, possibly arriving via Tintagel, suggesting yet again of links between Somerset and Cornwall. It was during Philip Rahtz's excavation on Glastonbury Tor that these important shards were discovered, and found to date from between the fifth and seventh century AD. They were thought to be storage jars used for transporting wine, olive oil, sauces and dry materials.

Rahtz speculates that 'whoever it was that brought them ... was presumably bringing not only wine or olive oil, but also other low bulk, high value materials such as spices or silk from the far east.'[xv]

He also believes that it was local leaders or kings, as well as ecclesiastical dignitaries, who were taking part in this trade, and that the findings on the Tor indicate earlier Christian habitation than at the Abbey site.

There certainly seems to be evidence that spiritual and cultural ideas also found their way into Britain via the Mediterranean traders. Many of the luxurious items that were imported to these areas are suggestive of a Byzantine mercantile culture.[xvi]

It would appear, then, that contact with these foreign traders undoubtedly shaped the emerging religious ideas in the British Isles. It is suggested that this is how the first Christian missionaries found their way to western Britain before St Augustine's arrival in Kent in the sixth century.[xvii] E.E. Barker observed that:

Glastonbury Tor. (Courtesy of Ken Macfarlane)

Earthworks at South Cadbury. (Courtesy of Ken Macfarlane)

William of Malmesbury's conclusion that missionaries may have reached the region in apostolic times remains as valid today as it was in the twelfth century. The commanding position of Glastonbury Tor and the largely marshy character of the land between it and the sea make it a likely choice as a landing-place, settlement and headquarters for early missionaries, who may have come by the ancient and well-known sea route from the Iberian Peninsula to the Bristol Channel.[xviii]

Even before the Romans arrived in Britain in 54 BC, there was an ancient trade route from the Mediterranean that accessed the island via the Severn Mouth.

It seems fair to conclude, then, that as early as the first and second centuries AD and into the following centuries there was a flourishing trade in goods to South West Britain from France, Northern Europe, the Middle East and Mediterranean, and that these merchants were often trading on quite a large scale:

Shutta, once a thriving port in the Looe Estuary, was capable of taking boats of considerable tonnage, providing a deep water anchorage for larger ships like the Roman merchantmen – used for carrying a variety of bulk commodities such as grain and metal ore.[xix]

St Joseph's Well, Glastonbury Abbey. (Courtesy of Ken Macfarlane)

The people who made their living from this trade were like bees carrying pollen to Britain, and the local inhabitants would have been involved in a rich pollination of ideas and beliefs – cultural, religious and scientific – that played a vital role in shaping the evolving ideas and beliefs of the people inhabiting the South West of England.

The Legends

> Legends often, perhaps generally, contain a germ of truth, and that the probable degree of truth can be fairly gauged by such considerations as source of origin; the localities where the legends had vogue; the likelihood or otherwise of the influence of careless legend mongers; and finally the result of applying to the legends the acid test of history and archaeology. I claim that the legendary visit of Our Lord to Britain, and to Cornwall in particular, comes through all these tests remarkably unscathed ... [xx]

From very early times, there have been legends telling that Joseph of Arimathea and some other disciples – including Mary Magdalene and Lazarus – came to Europe and England. Despite critics of the theory, it is still a widely held belief amongst many that Joseph, and others disciples who had fled the Holy Land with him, founded the first church in these Isles at Glastonbury. Controversial debate still rages amongst scholars on this subject, however, it has already been shown that from a very early date traders were coming to these Isles, and as Revd H.A. Lewis so eloquently said, 'The legend of Joseph of Arimathea could never be proved true. But could it ever be proved untrue?'

The legend concerning Looe Island and Cornwall is that Joseph of Arimathea came to Britain trading in tin, bringing with him the boy Jesus. One story recalls Jesus playing at the beach on the island. The Glastonbury legends are rather similar: Joseph originally visited the tin mines of the Mendips as a trader, bringing with him, on occasion, the boy Jesus. Some believe that during Jesus's 'lost years', when the Bible makes no reference to him, he was in fact acquiring knowledge at the 'Druidic Mystery School' in Glastonbury before his return to the Holy Land to complete his ministry. Whether this has any basis in reality or not has yet to be proven, but certainly the legend concerning Joseph's return to Glastonbury *after* Jesus's death and resurrection, and establishing the first church there seem to have a resonance of truth.

In the BBC Open University programme *Landscape Mysteries*, Professor Manning suggested that the shards of amphorae found on Glastonbury Tor pointed specifically 'to church contacts with Constantinople'.[xxi]

We know for certain that apart from the oral tradition, there were also writings that seem to bear out the idea of a visit by Joseph or other apostles to these Isles from as early as the second century; Eusebius of Caearea (AD 260-339) wrote in his *History of the Church*, 'some [apostles] have crossed the ocean and reached the Isles of Britain.'

Hilary of Poitiers, writing a little later (AD 300-376), claimed that 'the apostles had built churches, and the Gospel had passed into Britain.'

Both Hippolytus, documenting in around 170-23, and Tertullian, around 155-222, acknowledge the existence of Joseph of Arimathea, and note his importance at the time of Jesus's crucifixion and after his resurrection.

In his essay on Joseph of Arimathea, Daniel Agee points out that in the Gospel of Nicodemus, from the Apocryphal New Testament (*c*.150-255), Joseph is of vital importance in conveying the news of Jesus's resurrection to the Jewish Leaders.[xxii]

On his visit to Britain in 2011, former NASA scientist and Shroud expert Ed Prior gave a lecture in which he presented historical evidence to suggest that after the crucifixion of Jesus, Joseph of Arimathea, Mary Magdalene, Lazarus and other disciples disappear from the historical record. Prior concludes that this is because they fled Jerusalem for fear of their lives; this, he claims, was not merely because of their close association and sympathies with Jesus, but because they were in possession of his burial shroud, which they took as evidence of his resurrection.[xxiii] Jewish tradition deemed burial cloths as unclean, and if you valued your life you would not want to be found in possession of them.

Eusebius certainly connects Joseph to Jesus's burial and entombment, as do the canonical Gospels. By the fourth century, texts describing the Good Friday liturgy illustrate the vital role that Joseph played in Jesus's burial. This will be dealt with in further detail in chapter six.

A Tale Told: The Importance of Oral Tradition

Of our old historians in Britain, Nennius and Gildas are fragmentary to a degree, and never attempt to show how and when Christianity was first introduced into Britain. The Anglo-Saxon Chronicle, as its name suggests, deals principally with the Anglo-Saxons, and the compilers were probably woefully ignorant (as St Augustine was) of the early history of Celtic Christianity. Our own Celtic saints are little more than names, around which, as the late Canon Doble showed, reverence has woven beautiful and totally incredible legends. But as Canon Doble again insisted, they were real men and women who lived saintly lives in the districts their names commemorated. The reason we know so little about them is the same reason we know so little of Glastonbury and Cornwall in the first centuries of the Christian era. They lie in almost impenetrable darkness.[xxiv]

Modern scholars frequently dismiss the role of folk tradition and legend as of little or no importance to historical research. On the contrary, the role of such stories is often of great significance. Faithfully transmitted from one generation to the next, these mythologies have been drawn from a storehouse of ancient folk memory, stretching back hundreds, if not thousands of years. In most legendary sources there is undoubtedly a gem of profound truth, all too frequently hidden beneath layers of re-telling and embellishment.

What is revealed in these stories is an 'essence' of something vitally important to the seeker, it is often something that can be sensed, or glimpsed at, that goes far more deeply into the human psyche than the mere 'physical' or 'historical' record. We can often intuitively sense a tale to be true, even though we have no firm evidence for this knowledge.

Mythology takes us back to a time before things were 'written' in a physical sense; ancient Druidic and Platonic teachings are just two examples of ancient oral traditions transmitted in this form, though at one time it was one of the most important ways of transmitting knowledge for both the community and the family. Even today, most families have tales that are passed on, and almost certainly never written down!

Teachings passed from master to pupil can be termed as 'writing upon the soul'. The teaching of a master to his initiates was the way sacred truths were transmitted. It was considered that oral traditions were far more important than learning through reading.

A master's task was the care of the soul, and it was his task to transmit his knowledge in ways suited to the particular individual. Sacred myths were an important part of this teaching; they introduce the soul to his/herself.

Could it be that the legend of Joseph of Arimathea coming to Britain, or of *somebody* coming here, bringing with them *something* extremely Holy, was part of a sacred and ancient truth which was transmitted during the Middle Ages in the guise of the Grail legends? As John Cowper Powys says in *A Glastonbury Romance*:

Everyone who came to this spot seemed to draw something from it, attracted by a magnetism too powerful for anyone to resist, but as different people approached, they changed it's chemistry, though not it's essence, by their own identity, so that none of them had the same psychic effect ... Older than Christianity, older than the Druids, older than the gods of Norsemen or Romans, older than the gods of Neolithic men, this many-named mystery had been handed down to subsequent generations by three psychic channels; by the channel of popular renown, by the channel of inspired poetry, and by the channel of individual experience.

ENDNOTES

i Fortune, Dion, *Glastonbury. Avalon of the Heart*, p.23. (2000)

ii Lewis, Glyn, S., *Did Jesus Come To Britain?* Clairview (2008)

iii The Charter of Hasculf de Soligny (*c.* 1200)

iv W.M.M. Picken, Revd, *A Medieval Cornish Miscellany*

v Agee, D., *The Celtic Origins and pre Conquest History of Lamanna* (An essay, Looe Museum, 2006)

vi *Cornish Archaeology* no.33, p.125

vii William of Malmesbury (*The Antiquities of Glastonbury*) viii Olsen, Lynette, *Early Monasteries in Cornwall* (Boydell and Brewer, 1989)

iv Agee, Daniel, *The Celtic Origins and Pre-Conquest History of Lammana* (2006)

x Rahtz, P. and Watts, L., *Glastonbury Myth and Archaeology* (The History Press, 2009)

xi *Ibid*. p.178

xii Olsen, Lynette, *Early Monasteries in Cornwall* (Boydell and Brewer, 1989)

xiii Protheroe, M.J., *Somerset and Dorset Notes and Queries*. (Vol. xxxvii, part 374, September 2011)

xiv Alcock, L., *By South Cadbury, is that Camelot – Excavations at Cadbury Castle 1966-70* (Thames & Hudson, 1973)

xv Rahtz, P. and Watts, L., *Glastonbury Myth and Archaeology* (The History Press, 2009)

xvi Todd, M., *The South West to A.D. 1000* (1987), 2003

xvii Rahtz, P. and Watts L., *Glastonbury Myth and Archaeology* (The History Press, 2009)

xviii Carley, James P., *Glastonbury Abbey, p.xvii* (Gothic Image Publications, 1996)

xix Agee, Daniel, *The Celtic Origins and pre-conquest History of Lamanna* (An essay, 2006, Looe Museum)

xx Lewis, Revd H.A., *Christ in Cornwall and Glastonbury, the Holy Land of Britain. Part One* (www.ensignmessage.com/archives/christiancornwall.html)

xxi Protheroe, M.J., SDNQ. Vol. XXXVII. September 2011 (Part 374, p.73)

xxii Agee, Daniel, *Joseph of Arimathea – New Perspectives on Oral Tradition* (An essay, Looe Museum, 2006)

xxiii Prior, Ed, *Two lectures given at to accompany the Easter Shroud Exhibition at Wells Cathedral, Somerset* (2010)

xxiv Lewis, Revd H.A., *Christ in Cornwall & Glastonbury, the Holy Land of Britain. Part One* (www.ensignmessage.com/archives/christiancornwall.html)

2

HENRY DE BLOIS –
PRODIGY OF
THE TWELFTH CENTURY

He was deeply involved in the development of civil and canon law, in the writing of history and theology, and much else besides. As patron of the arts, Bishop Henry was matched by neither his episcopal contemporaries nor arguably by the kings in whose reigns he lived – Henry I, Stephen and Henry II.

Nicholas Riall, *Henry of Blois, Bishop of Winchester: A Patron of the Twelfth-Century Renaissance*

Born around 1090, Prince Henry of Blois was, by any standards, one of the most extraordinary and brilliant men of his time. Although the evidence supporting his achievements is somewhat fragmentary, and many of the historical sites associated with him have never been excavated, there still survives a significant amount of archaeological and documentary evidence from which we can piece together an understanding of his life and works. Curiously, for such an outstanding man, a complete study of Henry and his role in the twelfth-century renaissance has not yet been undertaken.

As a grandson of William the Conqueror, and brother of King Stephen of England, Henry came from a powerful, extremely wealthy and important aristocratic family – his father, Stephen Henry de Blois, was an important Crusader. Henry was a descendant of the line of families believed to have been

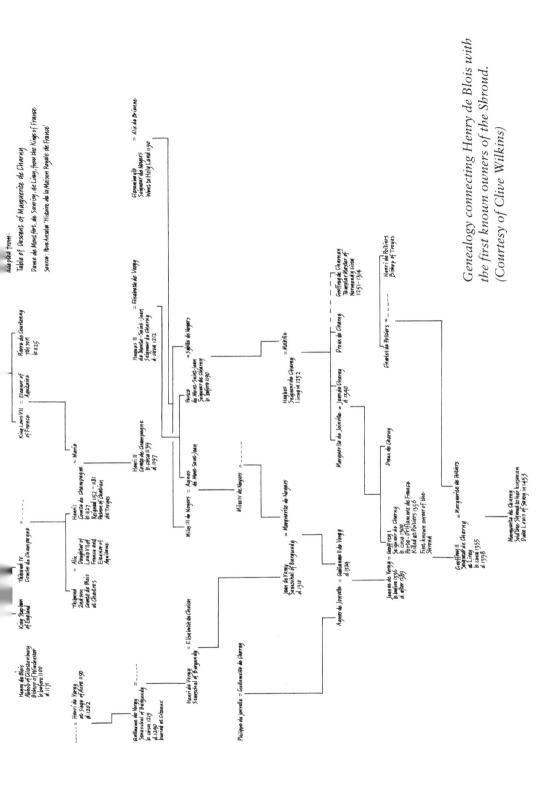

Genealogy connecting Henry de Blois with the first known owners of the Shroud. (Courtesy of Clive Wilkins)

in possession of what is today called the Shroud of Turin. These families are sometimes referred to as the 'Grail families' – families whose chosen task it was to be guardians of the Grail, whatever it may be. These included many of the aristocratic families of Europe, and the Blois family, through a series of inter-marriage, was connected to these. As can be seen from the genealogy (see page 37), the Blois family became connected by successive alliances to the de Charnay family, which included Geoffrey de Charnay, Master of the Knights Templar in Normandy, who was burnt at the stake after the Order was suppressed in October 1307. It also included another member of the same family, Geoffrey I de Charnay, who first exhibited the Shroud in Lirey in the twelfth century. We know for certain that the cloth Geoffrey displayed at Lirey was the same cloth we now call the Shroud of Turin. This shroud entered possession of the Dukes of Savoy in 1453, with whom it remained until the death of King Umberto II in 1983, when it passed into the hands of the Catholic Church.

Henry was educated at Cluny Abbey in Burgundy, where he was sent to train as a monk and church official. At this period in history, Cluny Abbey was 'the monastery to which many of the younger sons of both royalty and the leading members of the aristocracy were sent in the knowledge that these men would most likely enter the highest offices of the church across Europe ...'[i] He is believed to have arrived in England some time around 1120, under the patronage of his uncle, Henry I. It is known that the first position he was granted was as Prior of Montacute in Somerset.

In 1126, and still a young man, Henry was appointed Abbot of Glastonbury, then, just one year later, he was granted the position of Bishop of Winchester. He was also Lord of Taunton, where he built a priory outside the town walls.

These titles and the accompanying land made Henry one of the richest men in England.

With his appointments to Glastonbury and Winchester, Henry of Blois became master of very extensive estates lying across central and southern England. These estates, upon some of which stood castles and substantial houses begun by his predecessors, produced a prodigious income and made Henry of Blois one of the wealthiest churchmen of his time, and quite possibly the wealthiest individual in the realm during Stephen's reign. This wealth made viable the massive building programme the bishop initiated and carried out through his estates and, to a lesser degree, at the monastic houses of Glastonbury and Winchester.[ii]

This position would have given Henry greater political powers, and he was able to assist and influence his brother, King Stephen, in affairs of state. When Stephen was away from England, Henry largely controlled the governance of the country. Henry also sought to gain 'greater freedom for the Church over its own affairs, especially with regard to clerical appointments.'[iii] The Oxford Charter of Liberties (*c.* 1136), in which Henry was influential, helped him realise some of these ideals.

During his time at Cluny, Henry would have witnessed the celebrated re-building of the Abbey in splendid Romanesque style. This doubtless had a great influence on the young Henry as is illustrated by his architectural taste, examples of which can be seen today in buildings such as Glastonbury Abbey. Henry was famous for his extravagant aesthetic preferences in both architecture and the arts; at almost three feet in height, the illuminated Winchester Bible to be found on display at Winchester Cathedral, and the Winchester Psalter, now in the British Library, are considered to be amongst the finest examples of Romanesque art in Europe. Both are examples of Henry's remarkable creative influence during the twelfth-century renaissance. William of Malmesbury, of whom Henry was a patron and friend, commented that Henry was 'remarkable besides his splendid birth, for his literary skills'.

Twelfth-century tiled floor at Winchester Cathedral. (Courtesy of Ken Macfarlane)

Detail of the twelfth-century tiled floor at Winchester Cathedral.

The Tomb of Henry de Blois in the Quire, Winchester Cathedral.
(Courtesy of Ken Macfarlane)

Tournai Marble Font, Winchester. (Courtesy of Ken Macfarlane)

The church at St Cross, Winchester, commissioned by Henry de Blois.
(Courtesy of Ken Macfarlane)

At Winchester, the tiny and beautiful chapel of the Holy Sepulchre is finely decorated with Byzantine-style frescos, which strongly resemble the illuminations in the Winchester Bible and were most likely commissioned by Henry. Believed to be the finest examples of this style of decorative art in Britain, the paintings date to the 1200s and depict biblical scenes, such as the raising of Lazarus, Mary Magdalene and Jesus after the resurrection (*noli me tangere*), and Jesus's deposition and entombment, amongst others. We can surmise that there may well have been a similar chapel at Glastonbury.

What is of interest in the search for the origins of the Arimathean legend, and Joseph's association with the Shroud of Jesus of Nazareth, is that one of the frescos depicts him removing Jesus's body from the Cross and preparing him for burial.

Ian Wilson, Shroud scholar and author, observes that one scene in particular depicts 'Jesus being taken down from the Cross by Nicodemus and Joseph of Arimathea, with St John and Jesus's mother in attendance. Whoever the artist was, he painted behind St John and Nicodemus a third man carrying what can only be construed as a double-length shroud clearly designed to go over Jesus's head and down to his feet, exactly as we see in the case of our Turin Shroud.'[iv]

Wall painting illustrating a burial shroud being held up by a man.
(Courtesy of Ken Macfarlane)

Henry de Blois' Holy Sepulchre Chapel. (Courtesy of Ken Macfarlane)

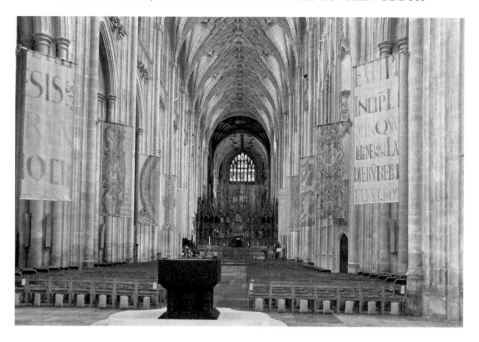

The nave, Winchester Cathedral. (Courtesy of Ken Macfarlane)

This fresco seems to indicate Henry's acknowledgement of the role played by Joseph of Arimathea at the death and burial of Christ. It would also suggest that he had knowledge of the appearance of the shroud (i.e. that it was a long, single sheet of cloth, which covered the back and front of the body, rather than the bandage-like wrappings of an Egyptian mummy). The Gospels tell us that Joseph provided the shroud, anointing oils and tomb for Jesus's body.

As a well-traveled man of noble descent, and as he is known to have had a particular interest in antiquities, we may justifiably ask the following: had Henry actually seen the Shroud in Constantinople where it was housed and displayed during this period in history? Or had he been inspired by stories of a mysterious bloodied cloth imprinted with the shadowy image of Jesus, which were being circulated by Crusaders and pilgrims returning from the East?

It is interesting to note that in approximately 970, Aethelwold, a dean at Glastonbury, later to become bishop of Winchester, wrote a liturgical drama known as the *Regularis Concordia*, which tells the Easter story of the women arriving at the sepulchre and discovering Christ's body gone. This drama prominently features the Shroud, which is held up for the clergy to see, as proof of Jesus's resurrection. Henry was surely familiar with this tradition, and we may surmise that the wall paintings he commissioned, and the

Easter drama, which was performed in the Holy Sepulchre Chapel, were an important way to transmit the story of Joseph and the Holy Shroud.

In 1130, the Anglo-Norman chronicler, Ordericus Vitalis, writing in the *History of the Church*, refers to the Mandylion of Edessa as the Shroud of Christ. Henry would certainly have been aware of Vitalis' chronicle, which states that:

> To him [King Abgar] did the Lord Jesus send the most precious linen, wherewith he dried the sweat from his face, and upon which the features of the Saviour appear, miraculously reproduced. It showeth to those who behold it the image and proportions of the body of the Lord.[v]

It is also of note that some traditions tell us that both Mary Magdalene and Lazarus left Jerusalem with Joseph to travel to Europe after Jesus's death; perhaps this is why they also feature on the wall paintings at Winchester. There may also have been a similar chapel built by Henry at Glastonbury; indeed, it would seem very likely considering that Glastonbury claimed a direct Arimathean connection and also to have the earliest Christian foundation in England – its very earth was seen as sacred. Unfortunately, most of Henry's incredible buildings at Glastonbury were destroyed in the great fire in 1184, just a few years after his death.

As previously mentioned, it is believed that the Winchester Chapel was originally used for Easter liturgical drama or rituals, which were probably similar in form to the 'Byzantine Rite' of the Eastern Orthodox Church. In this rite, one of the clergy takes the role of Joseph, and the *Epitaphios* (an elaborate copy of the full body image of the man on the Shroud) is carried along the nave and into a chapel, where it is laid upon an altar representing the sepulchre; the Epitaphios is then venerated by prostrating oneself three times and kissing the image.

This is surely reminiscent of the 'secret' traditions reputedly performed at the initiation ceremonies of the Knights Templar, in which they worshipped a shadowy image of a man on a linen cloth and kissed its feet three times. The Templars used to worship the Shroud with a liturgy that included kissing the wounds on the feet.[vi]

In the Byzantine Rite a special hymn is sung, whose words are: 'The most noble Joseph, when he had taken down Thy most pure body from the tree, wrapped it in fine linen, and anointed it with spices and placed it in a new tomb. Glory to the Father and to the Son and to the Holy Spirit, both now and ever, and unto ages of ages. Amen.'

The Lady Chapel, built on the site of the old church, Glastonbury. (Courtesy of Ken Macfarlane)

Doorway to the Lady Chapel. (Courtesy of Ken Macfarlane)

Romanesque twelfth-century carving at Glastonbury Abbey.
(Courtesy of Ken Macfarlane)

Glastonbury Abbey in the snow. (Courtesy of Alex Von Hellberg)

Glastonbury

As the centre of the monastic revival under Dunstan, Ethelwold and Oswald, the source from which the main stream of English mediaeval monasticism took its rise, Glastonbury held a unique position. Other abbeys and priories achieved importance for particular specific reasons – Westminster as the great royal foundation, St Albans for its thriving intellectual life, Canterbury for its metropolitan status – but Glastonbury was great merely because it was Glastonbury.[vii]

During Henry's abbacy at Glastonbury, the Abbey itself enjoyed something of a golden era. He is known to have carried out extensive rebuilding works at the Abbey, which helped to make it one of the finest and most important religious houses in the land. Many of the fine pieces of Romanesque carvings that can be seen at the Abbey and its museum today are a testimony to Henry's creative achievements and aspirations.

These and other extraordinary carvings evidently created by master masons are superb examples of the style with which Henry so frequently chose to decorate his extensive ecclesiastical buildings and palaces. He would undoubtedly have commissioned the finest craftsmen to work on these projects, and would doubtless have employed architects and other craftsmen from the Middle East as well as Europe. He was also known to have been a collector of antiques, important relics and classical sculptures.

The castles and palaces owned and frequented by Henry not only served as home to him, but also to the large retinue of staff, who would have been needed to maintain the significant estates.

The abbey at Glastonbury had an 'abbots deer park' situated on Wearyall Hill, which would have provided space for hunting and other recreational pursuits; indeed, Henry's contemporaries frequently chastised him for leading the life of a nobleman rather than that of a churchman, and he was criticized by his contemporaries for his extravagant tastes.

Further building works carried out by Henry at Glastonbury included a chapter house, cloister, bell tower, library, dormitory, lavatory, gatehouse, brewery and stables, as well as a building known as a castellum, thought to be Henry's residence. The castellum was the fortified palace that was chronicled by Adam of Domerham in 1200s, in which he describes it as 'a beautiful building'.[viii] Only the outline of this building can be seen today, amongst the ruins of the abbey, close to the Abbot's kitchen.

Glastonbury from Wyrall Hill. (Courtesy of Vicki Howd)

The Vetusta Ecclesia or Old Church

Henry would have been very aware of Glastonbury's important, ancient, regal and religious traditions. He would certainly have been familiar with the words in the *Life of Saint Dunstan*, written in the tenth century, which observe that:

> There was within the realm of King Athelstan a certain royal island known locally from ancient times as Glastonbury. It spread wide with numerous inlets, surrounded by lakes, full of fish and rivers, suitable for human use, and what is more important, endowed by God with sacred gifts. In that place, at God's command, the first neophytes of the Catholic law discovered an ancient church built by no human skill …

It is documented that the Lady Chapel at Glastonbury was burnt down in the fire of 1184, two years after Henry's death, and the remains of the existing building were built at a later date. However, Nicholas Riall convincingly argues that, 'The similarities of style and execution in the buildings at St Cross (Winchester) and the Lady Chapel at Glastonbury are such that we might judiciously question the chronicler's evidence'.

The Lady Chapel was constructed on the site of the *vetusta ecclesia* or 'Old Church', where legend tells us that the first church in Glastonbury was made 'without hands'.

In the fourteenth century, John of Glastonbury speaks of a continual habitation by twelve hermits right up until the fifth century. These hermits represented the twelve early Christian missionaries who were said to have originally settled at Glastonbury. John also writes that St Patrick became their eventual leader, and was given the title of first Abbot of Glastonbury in AD 433. Some scholars dispute this idea, suggesting it to be purely fictitious.

It is to be noted, however, that Ralegh Radford's excavations in the 1900s found evidence of several wattle oratories on the abbey site (see chapter 1). From these he deduced that the entire settlement on the Island of Glastonbury, including Beckery and its cemetery, 'may be regarded as part of the Holy City'.[x]

An early Anglo-Saxon chronicle, widely held to be of genuine origin, speaks of a 'Rex Domnonie' that is King of a Dumnonian tribe, who granted land on Inneswitrin to Glastonbury's *vetusta ecclesia*.

Professor Thomas argues that it was the land on the site of the ancient church at Glastonbury, which may have been granted by an ancient Dumnonian tribal King living at Tintagel, indicating yet again an early Christian tradition at both locations: 'Dumnonian Kings or sub-kings after AD 500, periodically on Tintagel Island, were together with their extended families and followers all Christian, nominal or devout'.[xi] It is believed that the king referred to in the charter was un-named because the charter was so ancient.

This evidence further confirms the tradition of a very early Christian community having been established at Glastonbury, which also presents itself in the merging of English and Celtic ideas at the abbey and its environs.

The cult of relics being brought to Glastonbury suggest that it was thought of as an especially sacred place, with objects coming from, among other places, the Celtic communities of Wales, Ireland, Cornwall and Scotland. Henry de Blois was one of the many notable relic-collectors known to have placed relics at Glastonbury; John of Glastonbury, writing in the fourteenth century, comments on the vast number of relics owned by the abbey, so many that 'there is no path through the church, cemetery or cemetery chapel which is free from the ashes of the blessed'.[xii]

We may hypothesize that some, if not most of the relics held at Lammana, when Henry de Blois acquired the place, found their way to the Mother Church at Glastonbury. Could it be that a piece of the 'Sovran Cloth' mentioned in Cornish mythology and Glastonbury legend was one of these relics?

It is also known that other relics of the Passion held at Glastonbury were a nail from the true cross, a piece of Jesus's robe, and part of the crown of thorns, which is now held at Stanbrook Abbey in Worcestershire. Further information about the significance of relics of the Passion is to be found in chapter 3.

In 1125, Henry commissioned William of Malmesbury to write a history of Glastonbury. In it he describes the 'Old Church', which was still standing at this time. William described it as being constructed of wattle and daub, and having a mysterious tiled floor, 'Under which I do believe some sacred mystery to be contained'. He also notes that there were many relics within, covering the altar and floor beneath.

Believed by the monks to be of great sacredness, they had preserved the entire building as a relic itself, and protected it by covering it with wooden planking and lead sheets. It was the centre of the Marian cult at Glastonbury

Certainly, Henry de Blois believed this location to be of unique importance, as he made a grant for a 'candle to burn night and day before an image of the blessed Virgin Mary in the Old Church at Glastonbury'.[xiii]

Henry was also patron of Geoffrey of Monmouth, whom he commissioned to write a history of the Kings of England in 1135. Being part Welsh, Geoffrey drew on his native Celtic legends, which included the story of King Arthur. This work became immensely popular in England and France, particularly due to royal interest in the Grail legends, particularly by Henry II and his wife Eleanor of Aquitaine.

Eleanor's daughter Marie, Countess of Champagne, was a patron of Chretien de Troyes, and Marie de France – believed to be Henry's half-sister – wrote the Lays of Tristan and Yseult and King Arthur. The popularity of the Arthurian stories spread rapidly through the courts of Europe, and they were known in such far away places as Alexandria and Constantinople.[xiv]

The Library at Glastonbury

I went straightway to the library, which is not open to all, to examine most diligently all the relics of most sacred antiquity, of which there is so great a number that it is not equally paralleled in Britain. Scarcely had I crossed the threshold when the mere sight of the most ancient books took my mind with an awe or stupor of some kind …

John Leland on a visit to Glastonbury Abbey, just before the Dissolution

As a man of great learning, Henry de Blois encouraged education and independent thought amongst the monks. By the middle of the thirteenth century, many monks attended university, and reading and study was a daily part of monastic life.

Henry was a great collector of books, and a patron of writers; consequently, the library and scriptorium of Glastonbury Abbey contained a large collection of important books. The main source of study was, of course, the scriptures, but, with time, reading and analysis of other types of literature was permitted.

During the Middle Ages, apart from aristocratic families, only a select few outside monastic settlements were able to read and write. This would have given the monks a sense of power and privilege; knowing things that many other people did not know or understand or have access to. As a consequence of this, the books in medieval monasteries were carefully guarded, and access to certain writings was restricted. Not all the books were to be read by all the monks – this was a way of ensuring that certain traditions were only known to the few, as was possibly the case with the Grail legends.

Professor James Carley observes that: 'Power, of course, involves the possibility of evil. The secrets revealed by the Word can destroy if misapplied. Faustus, the legends make clear, would have been in no danger without his books.'[xv]

It is thought that the widely read and accomplished Somerset-born scribe and illustrator, Dunstan (later St Dunstan), was responsible for establishing Glastonbury as a key centre for literature and study. He also played a key role in reviving monastic life based on the Rule of St Benedict:

> Which was successor in western Britain to the Irish communities of the Celtic world. Dunstan's revival spread far beyond the confines of his native county in the tenth century, and the active and generous support of successive members of the Saxon royal house made Glastonbury one of the richest monastic foundations by the time of the Norman Conquest.

Henry de Blois continued the tradition of collecting books for the Abbey library, and before 1171 arranged for the transcription of fifty books on various topics to be transcribed by the Glastonbury monks.[xvi] The Abbey was known to have a vast collection of eclectic writings, which attracted scholars from across the British Isles. John Leland noted that the library contained some ancient Christian documents as well as some very old histories of England.

John of Glastonbury, a chronicler of the fourteenth century, observed that several of the French Romances were kept at Glastonbury, 'In particular, the monks must have had access to *Perlesvaus* and the Vulgate cycle of Arthurian romances.'[xvii]

Romanesque twelfth-century carving, Glastonbury. (Courtesy of Ken Macfarlane)

It should, therefore, be of no surprise that in recent times rare fragments from a fourteenth-century copy of *Perlesvaus* were discovered nearby, at Wells Cathedral library (the fragment will be discussed at greater length in the following chapter). It doesn't seem too much of a leap of imagination to suggest that the copy may have originally come from Glastonbury Abbey and found its way to Wells sometime after the Dissolution.

ENDNOTES

i Riall, N., *Henry of Blois Bishop of Winchester: A Patron of the Twelfth-Century Renaissance*. p.3. (Hampshire County Council, 1994)

ii *Ibid*. p.9

iii *Ibid*. p.5

iv Wilson, Ian, *The Blood and the Shroud*. p.139 (Weidenfeld and Nicholson, 1998)

v Orderic Vitalis, *Historia Ecclesia*, III, lib.IX, 8

vi This evidence was found by Barbara Frale in the Paris Archives Nationale, J 413 n.25, un-numbered folios

vii Watkin, Dom. A. (Trans.), *Glastonbury Abbey Chartulary Vol.I.* (S.R.S. Vol.59)

viii Domerham, Adam, *Historia de Rebus Gestis Glastoniensibus* (Oxford 1727, Thomas Hearne)

ix Riall N., *Henry of Blois Bishop of Winchester*, p.18 (Hampshire County Council, 1994)

x Carley, J.P., *Glastonbury Abbey – The Holy House at the Head of the Moors Adventurous*. p.3 (Gothic Image Publications, 2003)

xi Protheroe, M.J., SDNQ, vol. xxxvii. Part 374. p.72

xii Carley, J.P., *Glastonbury Abbey*. p.129 (Gothic Image Publications, 2003)

xiii *Ibid*. p.10

xiv Weir, A., *Eleanor of Aquitaine*. p.137 (Random House, 1999)

xv Carley, J.P., *Glastonbury Abbey*. p.133 (Gothic Image Publications, 1996)

xvi Dunning, R., *Somerset Monasteries*. p.15 (Tempus, 2001)

xvii Riall, N., *Henry of Blois, Bishop of Winchester*. p.145 (Hampshire County Council, 1994)

3

THE QUEST BEGINS

Certainly something outstanding has been here [Glastonbury] for a very long time … whatever was here was special and treasured since at least the fifth century, and probably much earlier.

M.N. Palmer, *Sacred Britain*

The legends that tell of Joseph of Arimathea also tell us that he was in possession of something known as the 'Holy Grail' – an object connected with Jesus; and certainly Joseph's name is inextricably bound up with Jesus's burial and entombment, and particularly to the collection of his blood, and supposedly the vessel containing that blood.

In the case of the Glastonbury tales, Joseph was supposed to have taken two cruets containing the sweat and blood of Christ; these are depicted in the beautiful Victorian stained-glass window in St John's Church at Glastonbury.

Other interpretations as to the appearance of the Grail are: a chalice used by Jesus at the Last Supper; a *gradalus* (a large flat dish used for exotic dishes or meats); and, interestingly, a tile bearing the imprint of Jesus's face, which the Byzantines named the *Keramion*.

In the Anchiskhati Church in Georgia there is an icon known as the Ancha Icon, which is also known as the Keramion, or 'holy tile'. The image on the tile, which is a disembodied, bearded male head, was traditionally believed to have come into being miraculously, after the tile came into contact with the Holy Mandylion, or 'image made without hands'. This tile dates to the sixth century.

Ian Wilson suggests the Keramion, as a tile or slab, bore the image of the face on the Shroud, and he believes it was originally mounted above the gateway of the city wall at Edessa in Turkey. Edessa, now named Sanliurfa,

Crusading Knight and King, Glastonbury Abbey. (Courtesy of Ken Macfarlane)

was one of the earliest places known to be in possession of the cloth and one of the earliest places to become Christian. The people of Edessa converted to Christianity after their king, Abgar V, was miraculously healed by the image-imprinted cloth.

After Abgar's death in AD 50, the people reverted again to paganism, and all remaining Christians were persecuted. Wilson argues that the Shroud and tile were hidden in a special niche within the city walls to conceal their whereabouts, and there they remained, forgotten for hundreds of years, until severe flooding and destruction of the city revealed once more their hiding place.[i]

Chretien de Troyes, the first known author of the Grail legend, identifies the Grail as a large flat dish or platter holding a communion wafer, but he also speaks of other items from the Passion, such as the 'lance dripping with blood' – used to pierce Christ's side as he hung on the Cross. Chretien claims his writing was derived from an earlier source, as does Wolfram von Eschenbach, author of *Parsival*.

Wolfram's version of the story speaks of the Grail as a sone or tile, but he also claims that the Grail is not merely an incredible object, but a means of *concealing something* of great value. He also states that the Templars – in his words 'Templeisin' – are the guardians of this sacred object.

It is Robert de Boron, writing in about 1200, who specifically links Joseph of Arimathea with the Holy Grail; and the anonymous author of *Perlesvaus* identifies Glastonbury as one of the locations with Grail connections. Could it be that Joseph of Arimathea, or another disciple at perhaps a later date, brought with him to England a relic or relics of the Passion, including the Shroud, when the early Church became established there?

The one thread that binds all these Grail legends is the link with Christ's Passion, and, most importantly, they all allude to the importance of his blood, which was the ultimate sacrifice on behalf of mankind, for all time. This concept of the redeeming and transforming power of the Holy Blood is eloquently summed up in the words of Rudolph Steiner: 'The very moment when the blood flowed from the wounds of Jesus Christ upon Golgotha. All spiritual earthly relationships changed from this moment.'[ii]

It is to the story of Joseph bringing the two cruets to Glastonbury that we shall now return; what these objects may have been is open to conjecture. Perhaps the first thing that comes to mind is that perhaps there were *two* reliquaries brought to Glastonbury, containing the supposed blood and sweat of Christ. That is certainly a possibility, but there is, however, a very early source connecting Joseph to *two other* items containing Jesus's blood. An ancient Georgian manuscript dating to about 500 AD tells of Joseph collecting the blood of Christ on *two cloths*, the manuscript reads: 'But I Joseph climbed Holy Golgotha, where the lords cross stood and collected in a headband and a large sheet the precious blood that flowed from his holy side.'[iii] Orthodox tradition suggests that Joseph came to England in AD 37.

There are in existence today a head cloth, known as the Sudarium of Oviedo, which has been extensively researched by Mark Guscin, and a body-sheet known as the Shroud of Turin. Both these cloths are bloodstained with the *same* blood type.

When Jesus's body was removed from the Cross, his head and face were covered with a towel-sized cloth, much in the same way that an accident victim may have their face covered today. The head cloth was then removed from the body prior to burial, when it was wrapped entirely in the Shroud.

The sudarium is a much bloodier cloth than is indicated on the corresponding head area of the Shroud, as it is believed that it would have absorbed much of the blood from the head wounds; however, when the sudarium is overlaid on the Shroud, the bloodstains correspond. Scientists now largely agree that both cloths covered the same body within a very short space of time. Pollen residues discovered on both cloths indicate that they both came from the same location in Palestine.

There is a distinct possibility that whoever wrote the story of Joseph bringing two cruets of Jesus's blood to Glastonbury had heard of the earlier story, which told of blood being collected on two cloths. Certainly, from a very early date after the crucifixion, there were descriptions emerging of a cloth with a miraculous image upon it:

> Evidence begins in the fourth century for the survival in Edessa and later in Constantinople of a bloodstained burial sheet, widely considered throughout the Byzantine, Syriac Middle Ages as the very cloth Joseph of

The deposition showing Joseph of Arimathea (wearing hat).
(Courtesy of Ken Macfarlane)

Arimathea bought for the burial cloth of Jesus. This eyewitness literary evidence persistently relates that the sheet also bore the faint impression of Jesus' crucified body.[iv]

The image of Edessa was an icon bearing an image of Jesus face, supposedly 'made without hands' – that is without human intervention; it was not thought to be a painting, but a miraculous imprint.

Although most of the stories relating to the Holy Mandylion – as the image came to be known – refer only to the 'face of the lord', it is clear from the above quote, and other contemporary eyewitness accounts, that there was more to the cloth than a facial image; it's secret was that it bore the entire body image of the crucified Jesus, though this fact was only revealed to a select few people in special circumstances.

For most of the time the image remained folded in such a way as to only expose the face. It was then placed in a shallow golden casket or reliquary, with a trellis or lozenge border framing the face, so that it assumed a strange 'disembodied' appearance. The artifact was displayed infrequently and only to a chosen audience in special 'unfolding ceremonies':

> The Edessan clergy displayed the Icon amidst a deliberate mystique of secrecy vis-a-vis the congregation. Western travelers and crusaders in the Near East may reflect a confusion born of this secrecy and the Icons multiple terminology. Though they heard whispers of something intimately identified with or containing the portrait of the head and body of Jesus himself, the objects nature was unclear, and under the enhancing power of rumour, their reports may have led to the creation of different descriptions of the Grail.'[v]

It is not the purpose of this book to discuss in detail the Edessan Icon – many excellent and well-researched books have been written on this subject.[vi] What *is* of importance is that most experts now acknowledge that the image of Edessa or Holy Mandylion is the very same object as the Shroud of Turin.

We must remember that at the time the Grail legends were being written down, Crusaders, traders and pilgrims returning to the West were whispering of something very secret, with a likeness of Jesus upon it, and 'containing' his blood.

This mysterious object, which had been originally held at Edessa, was, in 944, reluctantly handed over to the royal treasury at Constantinople.

Shortly after it's arrival in the city, Gregory, the Archdeacon of Hagia Sophia Cathedral, was moved in a sermon to say that the Icon,

> ... was imprinted only by the perspiration of agony running down the face of the Author of life [and] has been embellished by the drops from his own side ... blood and water ... there, and here the perspiration and the figure ... the image and that which made the side to bleed were the same nature that formed the portrait.

Constantinople

Situated at the end of the Silk Road, Constantinople was founded by Roman Emperor Constantine I in AD 330 on the site of an ancient city named Byzantium. Constantinople was the capital of the Byzantine Empire, centre of the Eastern Orthodox Church, and the capital of Christian civilization for 900 years.

Constantinople was the wealthiest and largest city of the Middle Ages, and retained much of the culture of the ancient Roman empire; the roofs and domes of the buildings were covered in gold. It was a vast but well-organised metropolis, with an efficient government and its own navy. There were guilds for craftsmen and traders, and hospitals for the poor and sick. The Byzantines traded extensively, especially with the Venetians, and, as was noted in an earlier chapter, there was evidence of Byzantine trade with Britain.

The city was beautifully laid out with spacious open squares, often decorated with Greek and Roman works of art; it also had fountains and piped water. There was a huge hippodrome that could seat 80,000 spectators watching chariot races, and it was famous for its stunning mosaics, which decorated the city's many magnificent churches and monasteries, the most famous and breathtaking of these was the St Sophia Basilica. Apart from it's incredible buildings and fabled wealth, Constantinople had two of the world's most important treasuries; these were housed at the Blanchernae and Boukoleon Palaces, and the Pharos treasury; between them they held the most important relics known, and were reputed to contain all the relics of the Passion.

Visiting royalty, traders and pilgrims alike were dazzled and overwhelmed by the wealth and beauty of the city – no doubt also stirring up feelings of jealousy, resentment and greed. It is likely that royal guests, knights and others who were privileged enough to see the relics of the Passion, especially those who were privy to seeing the miraculous image of Christ, had thoughts of being able to obtain those treasures for themselves, whether by fair means or foul ...

In 1147, at the time of the second Crusade, Queen Eleanor of Aquitaine and King Louis VII embarked on a pilgrimage to Jerusalem. Their retinue included Master of the Knights Templar, Everard de Barre, and Henry, son and heir of Theobold, Count of Champagne. On their way to the Holy City, they stopped at Constantinople for twelve days. The Emperor of the city, Manuel Comnenus, and his wife, Irene, entertained them most lavishly during their visit, honouring them with the most extravagant hospitality. Comnenus provided the royal party with magnificent banquets, including musicians and entertainers. Elaborate food was eaten from silver dishes, and wine was drunk from glasses, and forks were used to eat with, which was unknown in the West at that time.[vii]

Whilst in Constantinople, some of the party, including the King and the Templar Grand Master, were shown the relics of the Passion, which were housed at the Blanchernae and Boukoleon Palaces. This would have included the Holy Shroud, which was kept at the Boukoleon Palace during that period.

In the spring of the following year, the entourage proceeded to travel to Antioch. By this time, however, things were already going badly wrong for the Crusaders; they were under attack from the Turks and huge numbers had been killed, while others were left injured and starving. Plague had broken out in the camp, and whilst thousands were left to die, many abandoned the mission as the Crusade began to collapse.

On a personal level, shortly after their arrival in Antioch, Queen Eleanor, famous for her intelligence, beauty and wealth, began an affair with her uncle, Raymond of Tripoli. This act was a dreadful scandal and understandably caused King Louis great hurt, anger and concern. Although they continued the journey to Jerusalem together, the marriage was almost at an end. On their return journey to France, the King's ships were attacked by the Byzantine navy, one ship was captured and its crew held hostage by the Byzantines. This was deemed an act of treachery against Christendom, no doubt sewing the seeds of resentment between the two nations, which, just a few years later, was to culminate in disaster for the Byzantines.

Not long after their return to France, Louis and Eleanor were divorced on grounds of consanguinity. It was Eleanor who instigated the divorce.

She wasted little time in finding a second husband in the figure of the handsome and impetuous red-haired Henry Plantaganet. He was only nineteen at the time, and destined to become Henry II of England. This marriage was a brilliant coup for the couple, because between them they owned vast tracts of land across England and France, from the borders of Scotland to the Pyrenees. This became known as the Angevin Empire.

In the years that followed, relations between Byzantium and the West were to become increasingly strained. It was against this background of religious zeal, the obsession with relics and the newly emerged Plantagenet dynasty, that the legends of the Holy Grail began to appear ... the Questing had begun.

The Shroud Vanishes

In October 1202, about 50,000 Crusaders set sail from Venice to embark on a fourth Crusade to try and re-conquer Jerusalem and win back the Holy Sepulchre. The army was mainly made up of French – many of whom were noblemen – and Venetians. The other half of the Christian army, which included the Knights Templar, were already waiting in the Holy Land after Pope Innocent III's call to arms, and, along with the Knights Hospitaller, they had organised a campaign plan.

From the very beginning of the Crusade, the omens were not good. Extreme financial difficulties, due to inadequate financial planning on behalf of the organisers of the Crusade, meant that there wasn't enough money to pay the Venetian shipbuilders for building the vast number of ships required for the campaign.

During November of that year, and only a few weeks into the venture, the Crusader fleet attacked Zara, which was part of the Hungarian Kingdom, and Christian. The Crusaders mercilessly looted the city, urged on by the Venetians, who hoped to re-take the territory for themselves. This was certainly an indication of the undisciplined behaviour of the army, but nothing compared with the horrors to come.

In 1203, due to an unexpected change of plan, and combined with an offer of financial assistance with the cost of the Crusade by the Byzantines, the Crusaders arrived in Constantinople in 1203 and set up camp outside the city walls. The political situation there was extremely unstable, and very quickly serious problems arose.

There had been uneasiness between the Roman Church and the Eastern Orthodox Church since the schism of 1054, and doubtless the Latin army, fuelled by greed and self-interest, saw an opportunity to seize for themselves some of the opulent wealth of the city. Some of the most important figures in the Crusade were invited into the city to see the coronation of the Emperor Alexis; this also included a tour of the Imperial Palace and its relics. And some of the promised financial aid was forthcoming, however, the situation escalated. Firstly, the Latin quarter of the city was attacked by Greeks, followed by the Muslim quarter of the city, which was set on fire by vandals from France and Venice. Due to the direction of the wind the fire took hold, and the entire Muslim area was burnt to the ground. However, some sanity prevailed, and for a time the situation temporarily calmed down.

During this time, a Crusader named Robert de Clari wrote about the public display of the Shroud at the church of St Mary of Blanchernae in Constantinople: 'Here was kept the syndoine (shroud) in which Our Lord had been wrapped, which stood up straight every Good Friday so that the features of our Lord could plainly be seen there.' De Clari also comments that the syndoine was preserved there in a 'dish'.[viii]

Present-day Shroud researchers have hypothesized that the Shroud could have been winched up by some kind of wooden device. It has been possible to reconstruct this device by following certain ancient crease marks on the cloth; these give a clue to how the Shroud was held up. The winch, very probably similar to the one used in Constantinople, would have enabled the Shroud to be hoisted into the air, gradually unfolding the cloth to expose the entire frontal body image, as de Clari describes.

The Byzantines loved to perform mystical and spectacular religious rituals, which would have been especially fitting for this rare and important ceremony. The Good Friday rite would doubtless have involved the use of subdued candlelight, incense, and special liturgical chants, probably very similar to the Eastern Orthodox rite performed at Easter today, the exception being that in Constantinople they possessed the genuine Shroud, which was on this and other special occasions removed from the golden reliquary where it was usually held. De Clari was amongst the few noblemen who were privileged to witness this unfolding ceremony.

The period of calm was short-lived and in 1204, after the overthrow of the newly crowned Emperor, the crusading army launched a full-scale and completely devastating attack on the city.

The attack was total, the city was completely ransacked; money, personal items and treasures were stolen or destroyed, women raped, churches defiled and their holy books were torn and burnt; the palaces were looted and their ancient artworks destroyed, and sacred relics stolen. Men, women and children lay dying on the streets. Constantinople was never to fully recover from this appalling devastation.

It was amidst all this chaos and confusion that the relics of the Passion, including the Shroud, disappeared. Crusader Robert de Clari commented that, 'No-one, not Greek, neither Latin knew what happened to the Shroud after the siege of the city.'

The Grail Emerges

A great many relics were clandestinely smuggled from Constantinople. Individual Crusaders either seeking to make a personal fortune or to enhance the status of their family line, would have placed the relics in their manorial churches as an attraction for pilgrims, and, importantly, the money they donated. Vatican archivist Barbara Frale observes that 'In no more than four years, the immense sacred treasury of relics kept in Constantinople was sent to Europe.' Fortunately, so precious were relics of the Passion that many were removed in specially made and sealed crates bearing 'a general passport and a certificate of authenticity that guaranteed their origin, a certificate bearing the golden seal of the Byzantine emperors.'[x]

King Louis IX of France bought the remaining relics of the Passion, said to include the crown of thorns and a piece of the true cross, at great cost in 1241. He commissioned the building of the magnificent church of St Chapelle in Paris to accommodate them.

What became of the Shroud in its golden casket after this atrocious attack and destruction? In a letter to Pope Innocent III, Theodore Angelos Komnenos, the nephew of the former Byzantine emperor, wrote in 1205:

> The Venetians appropriated the treasures of gold, silver and ivory, while the French did the same with the relics of the saints and the most sacred of all, the linen in which our Lord Jesus Christ was wrapped after his death and before his resurrection. We know that the sacred objects are preserved by their predators, in Venice, in France and other places, the sacred linen in Athens.

Whether these 'linens' were the Shroud or whether they were other cloths associated with the burial of Jesus, we cannot be certain, however, most Templar scholars agree that some time after the sack of Constantinople, the Knights Templar gained possession of the Shroud and were using it in their initiation ceremonies. Also, as Barbara Frale suggests, they were instrumental in spreading the 'cult of the Holy Face' across Europe.

In 1287, a young French Templar named Arnaut Sabbatier stated that at his initiation ceremony he had been led to a secret place that only the brothers knew, where he was shown the imprint of a man's body on a piece of linen cloth. He was told to adore him, and kiss the feet on the image three times.

Many historians suggest that the Templars acquired the cloth (probably at a very high cost) from Otho de La Roche, a Burgundian nobleman who

The Templecombe Panel. (Courtesy of Alex Meadows)

took part in the fourth Crusade. After the fall of Constantinople, he was granted position of Duke of Athens. Certainly at some period in history the Shroud appears to have been kept at Ray Sur Saone Castle, the seat of the La Roche family. To this day there is a chest on display in the castle (which is still owned by the family) that is said to have been the one that the Shroud was kept in while it was there. This chest is covered with a cloth that bears a painted image of the Shroud.

Clearly by the time the Shroud came into the possession of Otho de La Roche, it had been removed from the golden casket which had been its home for so many years at the treasury in Constantinople.

ENDNOTES

i Wilson, I., *The Shroud* (Bantam Press, 2010)

ii Steiner, R. (Ed. Gill McHattie), extract from *The Knights Templar: Influences from the Past and Impulses for the Future.* p.97

iii Wilson, I., *The Blood and the Shroud* (Weidenfeld & Nicolson, 1998)

iv Scavone, D., *Joseph of Arimathea, the Holy Grail and the Turin Shroud*. Shroud of Turin website, 1996: www.shroud.com/pdfs/n56part3

v *Ibid.*

vi Barbara Frale, Vatican archivist, and Ian Wilson, Shroud scholar, have written and
  researched the Shroud extensively and produced excellent books on the subject.

vii Weir, A., *Eleanor of Aquitaine* (Pimlico Random House, 1999)

viii Currer-Briggs, N., *The Holy Grail and the Shroud of Christ.* p.21 (ARA Publications,
  1984)

ix Frale, B., *The Templars and the Shroud of Christ.* p.155-6 (Maverick House, 2011)

x *Ibid.*

CHAPTER FOUR

GLASTONBURY AND THE GRAIL: MYTH OR REALITY?

In its long history in contact with our heroic pitiful human life it [the Grail] has succeeded in establishing itself both as a reality touched by the miraculous and as a miracle based on reality ... there are intimate correspondences between it and the traditions that reach us from both the extreme East and the extreme West. It changes its shape. It changes its contents. It changes its aura. It changes its atmosphere. But its essential nature remains unchanged, and even that nature is only the nature of a symbol.

John Cowper Powys, *A Glastonbury Romance*

In his verse 'The Romance of the History of the Grail', written between 1200 and 1210, Robert de Boron writes: 'The Grail is a reliquary which shall henceforth be called a chalice'.

This simple line encapsulates perfectly what is the most likely identity of a physical Grail: it had originally been a reliquary which held the blood of Christ soaked into his bloodstained shroud, but it became known as a chalice that held the blood of Christ, and this symbol is the one that remains today in the form of the Chalice of the Eucharist. The containers are different, but both held that element essential to the Grail – the blood of Christ. It is interesting to note that de Boron's patron was Gautier de Montbeliard, a French Crusader who was involved in the sack of Constantinople. Could it be that Montbeliard had told de Boron of the fantastical golden reliquary which held the bloodstained burial cloth of Jesus?

Glastonbury Tor. (Courtesy of Alex Von Hellberg)

The Grail legends tell a story – a story probably only intended to be understood by a select few. They *conceal* and *reveal*; the knowledge is hidden from the majority of people, but the clue to the Grail secret is there for all to see, 'hidden in plain sight'. When one perceives the Grail as a reliquary, in the form of a large, shallow container that held the most sacred Shroud of Christ, the legends become much more understandable.

Scholars have long known that the reliquary that held the Shroud whilst it was in the royal treasury at Constantinople was a shallow golden casket. The casket had a lozenge border, and the cloth was folded in such a way (doubled in four) as to reveal only the face, which appeared to be floating or disembodied. Tommasi points out that, 'The Templars used to own a precious icon covered in gold and silver, which featured the face of Christ, something analogous to the seals of Germany's Masters and the face on the Templecombe Panel.'[i]

There is certainly a growing body of scholars, including Noel Currer-Briggs, Daniel Scavone and Rex Morgan, to name but a few, who now believe that the Shroud and the Grail are probably one and the same. Noel Currer-Briggs has written an excellent and informative book on the subject, in which the Grail is clearly revealed as the reliquary that contained the Shroud.

However, the very thing that imbued the Grail with its transforming and miraculous qualities was the holy blood held within it, but the blood was not as liquid in the reliquary. It was soaked into a cloth – the Shroud.

When the body of Jesus was laid on the shroud that Joseph of Arimathea had provided, it would have been covered in blood from the appalling wounds he suffered at the time of the crucifixion, and this blood would have been transferred on to the cloth. Barbara Frale validly points out that when the disciples removed the Shroud from the tomb after the resurrection it would have been covered in blood that eventually coagulated to form a clotted mass, unlike the blood we see remaining on the Shroud today, which just has reddish-brown stains visible on the cloth that indicate where the wounds Jesus suffered were inflicted.

Frale believes that over succeeding centuries, small amounts of the clotted blood was scraped off, placed into special crystal phials and dispersed as relics (often at enormous cost) to certain kings, noblemen and churches. Today, however,

> ... nothing is left of the large, solid coagulations that the linen once bore, as if the stuff had lost, after unknown events, most of that thickened, solidified blood that originally stood in solid masses in relief on the sheet, like the crusts of so many wounds. In Constantinople, dispersed in the capital's over 1,000 churches, there were many reliquaries claiming to contain a part of the holy blood of Jesus, and many of them were taken to Europe by crusaders after the sack of 1204.[ii]

The same principle applied to the Shroud; we know that in the past tiny pieces of it have been removed – often no more than a few threads at a time – but they would have had the same sacred and transforming properties as the blood on the Shroud, because they had been in contact with the body of Christ. Frale continues: 'After the sack of Constantinople, several precious reliquaries containing tiny fragments of the Shroud of Christ had been sold across Europe, and even King Louis the IX the Saint had procured one for his reliquary in Sainte Chappelle.'[iii]

We must remember that such was the faith in the healing power of relics, that medieval man believed to touch a relic with another object meant that the object also became empowered. How much more powerful it was to touch or possess the very items that had been in contact with Jesus's body and his blood.

The Knights Templar reputedly had a large and important collection of relics, some of which were believed to have been kept at their preceptory at Templecombe, in Somerset. The Templars were believed to have been 'experts' in the identification of true relics, and their advice on the purchase of these objects was sought by churchmen and noblemen alike. Among their own collection was believed to be not only the Holy Shroud, but also a large piece of the true cross.

On occasion, tiny fragments of these items were removed, and given to, or bought by, wealthy, notable or worthy people. Many of these tiny relics were placed with, or attached to a larger piece of wood/cloth, which in turn, it was believed, became imbued with the power of the original.

This may be the reason why so many churches claimed to have a piece of the true cross or a fragment of Christ's burial shroud; somewhere in it's dim and distant history the relic would probably have been in contact with the original sacred object. As Frale observes:

> … one could not exhibit to the prayers of the faithful some thin wooden fibre, impossible to see once it was within the reliquary; so the holy fibre would be placed within a larger piece of wood, trying to select the same kind of material from which the original fragment had been taken. The more recent wood carrier became itself sacred by contact, the sliver once inserted in it would be lost and all but impossible to distinguish; but in all this there was no intent to deceive or defraud. Most relics of the Cross circulating in the Middle Ages were at least authentic in this sense, that it is derived from an authentic lift of the material from the greater relic.[iv]

A possible example of this concerns a certain reliquary at St Vitus' Cathedral in Prague, which claims to contain a part of the burial shroud of Christ. This brownish-coloured piece of cloth was carefully examined in 2001, but it turned out to be made of silk, not linen, so therefore it could not be a piece of the Shroud of Turin. What is interesting, though, is that after being taken from Constantinople, the Shroud was consistently wrapped in silk for protection. A plausible theory for the belief that the relic in Prague was a shroud relic is that the silk may have actually wrapped the Shroud at some point in its history, thus becoming a relic in itself.[v]

Knight Crusader at Glastonbury Abbey. (Courtesy of Ken Macfarlane)

St Patrick's Chapel and Holy Thorn, Glastonbury. (Courtesy of Ken Macfarlane)

Similarly, the 'shroud relic' at Toledo Cathedral in Spain was found to be a piece of silk taffeta, suggesting once again that it may have acted as protection for the original Shroud at some point in its history. Both these pieces of silk, if they indeed did wrap the true Shroud, would have been in contact with Jesus's blood, becoming sacred in their own right.

The Sovran Cloth at Glastonbury

In the library of Trinity College, Dublin, is a very important and ancient book called *The Book of Armagh* or *The Canon of Patrickvi*, which is believed to date from at least the ninth century, possibly earlier. The book is a transcript of earlier documents and is sometimes said to have belonged to, or been influenced by St Patrick, who, as was noted in an earlier chapter, was said to have founded a monastic settlement on the site of Glastonbury's Old Church.

Interestingly, the book speaks of a relic of 'the most holy blood of Jesus Christ, the redeemer of the human race, in a sacred linen cloth, together with relics of the saints, where rest along with Patrick the bodies of holy pilgrims ...'

Could a piece of Jesus's Shroud have been held at Glastonbury – brought to the place by Patrick? And is this why the legends of Joseph and the springing of Christianity arose there?

Reverend H.A. Lewis carried out research into the oral traditions associated with the legends of Joseph of Arimathea and Jesus at Lammana, Cornwall. He interviewed an elderly lady who had grown up in nearby Port Looe and Portallow. She spoke of her memory of 'a piece of old cloth, treasured by a family from Portallow', which they claimed was a 'part of the cloth in which our Saviour's body was buried'.[vii]

This may have been one of the holy relics reputedly concealed in the chapel at Lammana, which were dispersed before the Dissolution to prevent them being taken from Cornwall or falling into the 'wrong hands'. If this is the case, it is certainly possible that the cloth may survive, even today, in the hands of some notable Cornish family.

Equally plausible is the idea that a cloth fragment was taken from the Mother Church at Glastonbury to Lamanna, or vice versa. There is some further curious evidence for this, which should not be dismissed. In 1908, Somerset historian and vicar, Reverend Thomas Escott, wrote concerning the 'portables' of Joseph of Arimathea:

> Chief amongst these was the linen that had once covered the Divine Body, and which he destined as a future covering for his own remains. In the present writer's childhood, diminutive fragments of this material were, to Glastonbury, what pieces of the Cross are to Continental shrines.[viii]

This enigmatic phrase indicates a survival, until comparatively recent times, of fragments that were believed to have come from the Shroud of Christ. Moreover, the suggestion that the fragments inspired reverence comparable to those of Continental shrines would seem to imply that there was some form of 'Cult of the Holy Shroud' at Glastonbury itself. Historian Paul Ashdown suggests that 'it would seem that Glastonbury once laid claim to having its own Holy Shroud.'[ix]

It is tempting to think that this material was indeed part of the 'sacred linen cloth' that the *Book of Armagh* claims was brought here by St Patrick himself, or dare we even venture to think that it was brought to Glastonbury by Joseph of Arimathea, at the foundation of the ancient church?

Ashdown observes that there was no Catholic place of worship in Glastonbury in the mid-nineteenth century, and that Somerset was 'staunchly Protestant at this date', which would have made a Cult of the Holy Shroud 'unthinkable'. Nonetheless, perhaps Escott's childhood memories were of Shroud fragments venerated in some private shrine, or perhaps even being put up for sale.[x]

It would seem most likely that the fragments were venerated in a family chapel somewhere in Somerset. This would reflect the memory of the elderly lady from Portlooe, in which the fragments surviving in Cornwall were in the care of 'a local family', for it would seem apparent, even in the nineteenth and twentieth centuries, that the value of these artifacts would have been realised, and, once there, may have been great reverence for them, as there is for other relics in Continental cathedrals and churches.

Of course the question remains – were these fragments tiny pieces of the artifact we now call the Shroud of Turin, or were they fragments of some other cloth that had touched the Shroud, such as was probably the provenance of the silk cloths in Toledo and Prague?

Unless the fragments re-appear and can be examined and dated, we have no definite proof either way. Therefore, apart from the *Book of Ardagh*, is there any other pre-nineteenth-century evidence that a cloth, or fragments of a cloth purporting to be Jesus's shroud were held at Glastonbury, and could this very cloth be the reason that the legends of the Holy Grail became attached to the place?

Ashdown has identified a Glastonbury verse, the 'Lyfe of Joseph', thought to have been written in 1502, which tells of Joseph and the Holy Thorn. It contains the words:

'If thy be Jhesu,' sayd Joseph, 'that here doth stand'
Gyve me thy richest treasour of this land,
The cloth that is called the Sedony.'
Jhesu led hym to the sepulture & there it fonde;
'Holde Joseph,' sayd Jhesu, 'that couerture of my body'.[xi]

This verse indicates an early connection between Joseph, the Shroud and Glastonbury, and the possibility of the acknowledgement of shroud fragments revered in the town. Stained-glass windows in St John's Church in Glastonbury and All Saints' Church in Langport show Joseph holding a cloth, as well as the two cruets. Joseph is frequently displayed with the Shroud draped over one shoulder and across one arm, as is the case in the window at Langport church.

A very important clue to the mystery associated with the Shroud is revealed in the twelfth-century Grail legend *Perlesvaus*, or *The High History of the Holy Grail*.

In the chained library at Wells Cathedral, only six miles from Glastonbury, are to be found fourteenth-century fragments of a copy of *Perlesvaus*.

Professor James Carley comments that these form an important witness to the circulation of this legend in England. Although the author of the book is unknown, it has been suggested that someone with an intimate knowledge of Glastonbury Abbey and the surrounding area composed it. Undoubtedly there seems to be a connection between Glastonbury and *Perlesvaus*, as at the end of the book the author informs us:

> The Latin from whence this history was drawn into Romance was taken in the Isle of Avalon, in a holy house of religion that standeth at the head of the Moors Adventurous, there where King Arthur and Queen Guinevere lie, according to the witness of the good men of religious that are therein, and have the whole history thereof, true from beginning to end.

There are various ideas put forward as to the identity of the author, ranging from a Knight Templar suggested by Katherine Maltwood, to Hank Harrison's suggestion of Henry de Blois, or, more plausibly, a Welsh or Glastonbury scribe. The true author remains elusive.

The importance of the Shroud in this version of the Grail story is revealed by the 'quest' of Perceval's sister, Dindrane, in which she must find the 'Sovran Cloth' in the Perilis Chapel, a terrifying and haunted place. Once within, her task is to cut a piece from the cloth. The quest is for her alone; it is, she says, the only way in which 'the knight that warreth upon us' will be overcome. It is her task to retrieve for him a piece of the cloth, which is 'the most holiest, for our Lord God was covered therewith in the Holy Sepulchre, on the third day when He came back from death to life.' The first time Dindrane enters the Perilous chapel,

> … she seeth above the altar the most holy cloth for the which she was come thither, that was right ancient, and a smell came thereof so sweet and glorious that no sweetness of the world might equal it. The damsel goes toward the altar thinking to take the cloth, but it goeth up into the air as if the wind had lifted it, and it was so high that she might not reach it.

Two very interesting features with some bearing on historical reality are described in this passage. Firstly, Dindrane notices the smell of the cloth: this is a phenomenon that was frequently noted by many of those who had seen and touched the Shroud of Turin – it is said there still lingered the smell of the myrrh, aloes and perfumed oils with which the body had been embalmed.

This is not merely imagination, as modern archaeologists have noted that sometimes upon unwrapping the remains of Egyptian mummies, there still remains a faint, sweet odour of the herbs and embalming oils used to preserve the corpse.

Modern scientists have identified traces of burial herbs on the Shroud of Turin, herbs that were customarily used in Jewish burials of the first century.

In 1201, the keeper of the royal treasury at Constantinople, Nicholas Mesarites, gave an account of the burial Shroud of Christ, commenting that 'it was made of linen, and still smelt of myrrh.'[xii]

The second point of interest is that the cloth is raised into the air, as it was in a part of the Byzantine rites practiced in Constantinople, when the Shroud was mechanically 'raised into the air' to slowly reveal the entire image of the Lord.

Dindrane's final visit to the chapel proves more successful. She prays,

'Lord, grant it be your pleasure that I may have it, for love of the knight by whom it was set in this chapel; sith I am of his lineage it ought well to manifest itself in this sore need, so it come according to your pleasure.' Forthwith the cloth came down above the altar, and she straightway found taken away therefrom as much as it pleased Our Lord she should have. [xiii]

Dindrane was able to remove a portion of the cloth because she was of the lineage of Joseph of Arimathea. Was this an allusion to the very piece of cloth that was kept as a relic in Glastonbury? It also hints at a special family lineage, who appear to be privy to certain secrets, which, some suggest, were known about in Glastonbury. Carley observes that the Grail legends were associated with 'aristocratic households' rather than ecclesiastical institutions. Certainly by the time *Perlesvaus* was written, the Shroud was probably in the possession of the Knights Templar, and the mysterious author of the legend would certainly have been aware of the mystique attached to it and the other relics of the Passion. *Perlesvaus* also tells of the 'circlet of gold', which is the crown of thorns. In 1191, the monks from Glastonbury supposedly 'found' the burials of Arthur and Guinevere. Modern scholars tend to be of the view that it was an elaborate hoax on the part of the monks, as a fund-raising exercise to gain funds from pilgrims to aid with rebuilding parts of the Abbey after the great fire of 1184, which destroyed most of Henry de Blois' great building works, including the library. Carley comments that the monks may have circulated the news of the discovery of the burials in 'oral form' on the Continent before

The site of Arthur and Guinevere's tomb, Glastonbury. (Courtesy of Ken Macfarlane)

the legend was written down. However, he also notes that Richard Barber suggests that news of this incredible discovery may also have been circulated 'in a kind of newsletter'.[xiv]

It is not the purpose of this book to argue for or against this idea, but what is of interest is that the skeletons found were buried in hollowed-out tree trunks, which is a very ancient form of burial, one that medieval monks certainly wouldn't have been aware of, and so, therefore, could not have deliberately replicated. The question remains then: whose burial was it?

The main thing is that the people of the time *believed* that the burials were Arthur and his Queen, and that is how the story was chronicled.

A Fragment of Perlesvaus at Wells Cathedral Library

(Based on a study of the fragments by Professor James Carley)

Preserved in the Chained Library at Wells Cathedral, a mere six miles from Glastonbury, are two ancient fragments of the *Perlesvaus*. Their remarkable survival is due to the fact that they had been used as binding for a register written by the dean of Wells, William Cosyn, between 1499 and 1525. The dean had noted that the binding contained two folios of Arthurian Romance, but James Carley understands that he was the first scholar to identify them as coming from *Perlesvaus* or *The High History of the Grail*. Carley observes: 'The script can be dated to the first half of the fourteenth century and the hand is clear and well formed.'[xv] He also comments that 'the worthlessness of the fourteenth-century Romance by sixteenth-century standards is what guaranteed its survival'; if the book hadn't been used for binding purposes it would almost inevitably have disappeared.[xvi]

Over the years, further fragments have turned up at other locations, and it is suggested that they all originated from north-eastern France. Some scholars believe that Glastonbury was the intended setting for *Perlesvaus*, and that the original French text was copied and adapted by an Anglo-Norman scribe. Carley observes:

> Both the internal passages and the colophon make it abundantly clear even to the most hardened sceptic that the author of *Perlesvaus* must have had Glastonbury in mind when he described Avalon, and that he must, therefore, have heard about the famous Arthurian excavation in 1189/91.[xvii]

He further notes that the exhumation of King Arthur is not mentioned in any Continental document until *after* the latest date possibly acknowledged for the composition of *Perlesvaus*; this, he believes, is what indicates that the Romance may have been written in Britain. Furthermore, he goes on to refer to 'internal allusions which seem to show a very precise knowledge of the Glastonbury landscape'. These features include observations of the Tor, the Old Church, and the Chalice Well.

He acknowledges that the author may have merely read the 'monks newsletter', which Richard Barber believes may have circulated on the Continent informing people of the discovery of King Arthur's tomb, but suggests that the descriptions in the Romance appear to infer a more intimate connection with Glastonbury.[xviii]

William Albert Nitze (1876-1957) was another scholar who had studied and edited *Perlesvaus*. Nitze was a brilliant scholar who, among his many other achievements, was the Head of the Department of Romance, Language and Literature at the University of Chicago. He had also studied early French literature and Arthurian Romance. Nitze believed that an early Latin source of *Perlesvaus* could have existed in the library at Glastonbury Abbey, from which the anonymous author of the Romance found his inspiration, and which was hinted at in the Romance.

The Chapel Perilis and the Perilis Bridge

Wyrall, or Wearyall, Hill is reputed to be the spot where Joseph of Arimathea and his weary followers first set foot on Glastonbury soil. This is where, as legend recounts, he planted his staff, which miraculously sprouted and flowered at Easter and Christmas and became known as the Glastonbury Thorn. Sadly, this tree has been vandalized and destroyed in recent times, although cuttings taken from it still survive at various locations in the town, and they do indeed flower at Christmas and Easter. It is also known that the

The Holy Thorn on Wearyall Hill, reputedly struck from Joseph's staff. (Courtesy of Vicki Howd)

The Pons Perilis, or Perilous Bridge. (Courtesy of Ken Macfarlane)

tree originated from a Middle-Eastern species of thorn. A cutting from one of the trees is presented to the Queen every Christmas, representing, perhaps, the remembrance of an ancient royal lineage …

On the far western extremity of Wyrall Hill, close to the then ancient island of Beckery, and near the modern road to Street, is a decidedly unimpressive bridge over the River Brue, which still bears the romantic name 'Pons Perilis', or Perilous Bridge. The existing bridge is largely Victorian, being constructed between 1826 and 1828, although archaeological excavations conducted by John Morland in 1881 suggest that the bridge may have been Roman. Furthermore, Morland noted that, 'When drains were being laid in the fields east of the causeway, an ancient road was discovered which had long been buried and forgotten.'[xix] This 'ancient road' was excavated some forty years later in the early 1900s, when an archaeological dig was overseen by his grandson, Stephen, who carefully examined the site of a section of track running parallel with the modern road to Street. This excavation project found evidence of both a medieval bridge and causeway, and traces of a much more ancient structure beneath. It is thought the medieval work was completed in the twelfth or thirteenth centuries.

The Chalice Well, where the 'Grail' or Cup from the Last Supper was reputedly hidden. (Courtesy of Alex Von Hellberg)

Furthermore, Stephen Morland's excavations revealed an even earlier structure; this was a causeway, a packhorse track for men and horses, and a wooden bridge, which he believed to be Roman. Morland believed the early structure to be Roman on account of finds of Roman pottery at the site, which were comparable with pottery shards found higher up Wyrall Hill.

However, Richard Brunning recently excavated the causeway; this included taking samples of the wooden pile making up the track for radiocarbon dating. The samples indicated that the trackway was seventh or eighth century. Brunning found no evidence of Roman work, suggesting that the pottery fragments found by Morland were just randomly scattered there. He suggested there was a possibility that an earlier structure had existed before the early medieval causeway, but to date no evidence has been found to suggest this.[xx] The seventh/eighth-century date confirmed by Brunning coincides with other important evidence of settlement at Glastonbury, such as the construction of the Old Church. Another important discovery made by Morland's team was that of a medieval iron boot spur, believed to be of twelfth-century origin – possibly from the time of Richard I.

It was Richard's parents, King Henry I and his wife Eleanor of Aquitaine, who first instigated a search for the remains of King Arthur at Glastonbury. Records suggest that Richard was in possession of what was believed to be Arthur's magical sword, Excalibur, which was supposedly found at the time that King Arthur's tomb was 'discovered' by monks in 1191. Richard is said to have exchanged the legendary sword for nineteen ships, as part of an agreement with King Tancred of Sicily.[xxi]

Legend tells us that the Perilis Bridge was the very bridge from which the mortally wounded King Arthur threw Excalibur into the river, before being taken to his final resting place in Avalon.

The name Perilis Bridge appears to be named straight from medieval Arthurian legend, though some evidence exists for its construction in much more ancient times; but what of the Perilis Chapel which housed the Sovran Cloth?

It is usually suggested that this chapel was to be found close by the Abbey site; however, would it not be more likely that the Perilis Chapel would be located close to its namesake, the Perilis Bridge?

Morland's excavations suggest that the ancient river once divided in two under the Pons Perilis, one branch of it flowing across the moor, another meandering close to Beckery Island and its ancient chapel.[xxii] The author contends that this is a much more likely location for the legendary Perilis

Chapel mentioned in *Perlesvaus*, and a much safer place to keep a sacred relic such as the Sovran Cloth, or Holy Shroud.

ENDNOTES

i Frale, B., *The Templars and the Shroud of Christ*, P.162. Ref. Tommasi (Maverick, 2011)

ii *Ibid.* p.250-1

iii *Ibid.* p.242

iv *Ibid.* p.225-6

v Duncan, H., *The Shroud Relic in Prague* (www.shroud.com/pdfs/n74/part 7.pdf)

vi Codex Armachanus (The Canon of Patrick) Irish Latin M/S. Trinity College Library, Dublin

vii Lewis, H.A., *The Christ Child at Lammana*, Looe Old Cornwall Society

viii Escott, T.H.S., *Somerset: Historical, Descriptive, Biographical*, p.12

ix Ashdown, P., Downside Review, p.174. 2003

x *Ibid.*

xi *Ibid.* p.188

xii Currer-Briggs, N., *The Holy Grail and the Shroud of Christ*, p.30. (1984)

xiii Dindrane was of the lineage of Joseph of Arimathea

xiv Carley, J., *A Fragment of Perlesvaus at Wells Cathedral Library*. (This can be seen by appointment at the Chained Library in Wells Cathedral.)

xv *Ibid.* p.1

xvi *Ibid.* p.2

xvii *Ibid.* p.4

xviii *Ibid.* p.5

xix Morland, J., SAHNS Proceedings (xxvii, ii 43-50)

xx Conversation with Richard Brunning regarding excavations of the causeway (April 2012)

xxi Weir, A., *Eleanor of Aquitaine*, p.138 and p.271 (Pimlico, 2000)

xxii Morland, J., *The Roman Road, Pons Perilis and Beckery Mill: A Regional Survey*, Holy Trinity, Street and Walton (www.Street and Walton.co.uk/history_brue. html)

5

DID THE SHROUD COME TO SOMERSET DURING THE MIDDLE AGES?

As religious knights sworn to the upholding of Christianity and protectors of the route to and from Jerusalem, they knew the tradition of the connections between Joseph of Arimathea and the constant quest of the Knights of King Arthur for the Holy Grail, whatever it might have been, in the district where, incidentally, is the site of the greatest claim to being King Arthur's Camelot, namely South Cadbury Hill, a mere six miles from Templecombe village.

Rex Morgan, 1987[i]

This chapter is largely based upon discussions I have had with, and research papers given to me by Shroud scholar and international author Rex Morgan.

Templecombe

Templecombe is a village in Somerset close to Cadbury Castle, which, due to the archaeological evidence of an important Dark Age settlement, many believe to be the site of Arthur's legendary Camelot. Certainly, it must have been the stronghold of a powerful local warlord.

Although there is some confusion as to when exactly they acquired the land, Combe was definitely in the possession of the Knights Templar by 1185, which was the date of the Templar inquest or survey of Templar lands in Somerset. (This is dealt with in further detail in my previous book.[ii])

The Templecombe Box. (Illustration by Rebecca Gryspeerdt)

Certainly, not long after they acquired Combe, the Templars established a preceptory, or commandery at the location, and it became known as Combe Templar, or Templecombe. Templecombe became a place of great significance for the Templars and it eventually overtook the Bristol preceptory in importance, becoming their main headquarters in the South West of England.

Templecombe is situated close to the Roman road the Fosse Way, and is conveniently situated between the ports of Poole and Bristol, which was essential for the transporting of knights, horses, pilgrims and trading goods from England to the Continent and beyond. The Templecombe preceptory was, in its time, a place of wealth and renown, where visiting churchmen and pilgrims alike stayed at the preceptory and hostelry, often en-route to the Holy Land. In his book,

The author at South Cadbury: King Arthur's Camelot? (Courtesy of Ken Macfarlane)

Somerset Villages, Paul Newman also suggests that it was a location where important relics were safely stored. Unfortunately, due to bombing raids in the Second World War, much of the evidence of Templar occupation, and indeed many of the old and interesting properties, were destroyed. Despite a three-day archaeological 'dig' by Wessex Archaeology for Channel 4's *Time Team* programme, most of the former preceptory site now lies under a housing estate.

One remarkable survival of the Middle Ages is the so-called 'Panel Painting', which was accidentally discovered by an elderly lady named Molly Drew in 1944.

Mrs Drew relates that she went into her wood store one day, and noticed some of the ceiling plaster on the floor. On looking up, she was startled to see a face looking down at her! The face was securely wired into the ceiling of the wood store, and had been covered in lathe and plaster; clearly, it had been deliberately and carefully concealed in the ceiling for some reason.

Mrs Drew and others removed the painting, which was covered in cobwebs and dirt. The wood store itself was a room attached to her cottage, but on a lower level than the rest of the property, with a dirt floor and only a curious circular stone 'porthole' for light. The cottage was later identified by local historian Audrey Dymock Herdsman as being the 'priest's house', minutes away from the main preceptory buildings. It was believed that the image could have been concealed in the ceiling for hundreds of years.

Mrs Drew originally described the panel as being very brightly coloured with vivid blues and reds, with golden stars surrounding the image, which was believed to be the face of Christ.

Unfortunately, the local Bishop decided to try and clean the panel, and scrubbed it in the bath with Vim! This all but removed the brilliant colours, and all that remains today is a very muted image, and no evidence to the naked eye of the golden stars. Whilst being 'stabilised' by conservator Eve Baker in 1955, remnants of the stars were found, and evidence of the bright blue pigment azurite. Further restoration in 1980 by conservator Anna Hulbert found minute traces of verdigris (bright green) and vermillion (red). Clearly the picture was similar in colour to the vibrant Icons of Byzantium, and very different to the subdued sepia image that can still be seen today. The panel, which measures 4 feet 9 inches wide, by 2 feet 9 inches high, and 2 feet deep, was put in the local church in 1956, where it received little serious attention until recent times.

In 1978, historian and Shroud scholar Ian Wilson drew attention to the artefact with his theory that the painting was a direct copy of the face of the Shroud of Turin. This theory was borne out by Alan Whanger of Duke University, when he carried out a 'polarising overlay' technique. This technique is frequently applied to images which are thought to be based on the Shroud, to see how many features of similarity occur. The panel painting revealed 125 points of similarity to the Holy Shroud.

A carbon-14 dating was carried out, which concluded that the wood for the panel was of medieval date, cut between approximately 1280 and 1310 – during the time of Templar occupation at Templecombe. Wilson concluded that it could, therefore, have been one of the mysterious 'heads' (now believed to be copies of the face on the Shroud) that the Templars were accused of venerating at the time of their suppression. A television documentary entitled *A Head of Time* followed this discovery, which propelled the panel from obscurity into the spotlight, and ever since it has drawn Templar enthusiasts, sceptics, and other curious parties from around the world to this obscure Somerset village.

In 1987, historian, international author and Shroud scholar Rex Morgan revisited Templecombe to continue his previous work on the Templecombe Panel. Since its discovery, the artefact has always been known as a 'panel painting', however, with fresh insight, Rex and his team realised that the panel may reveal a very different secret, one that was more profound and

The Templecombe Panel. (Courtesy of Alex Meadows)

had greater implications to all those who would seek to discover the true identity of the Grail.

At the time of its first discovery, various people had suggested that the panel may have been the lid of a vestment box, and this, Morgan believed, was the key to its true nature.

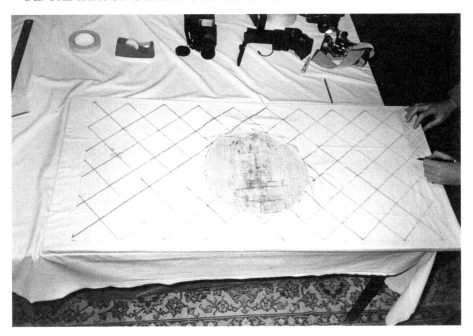

Shroud face and trellis, grille or lozenge covering. (Courtesy of Rex Morgan)

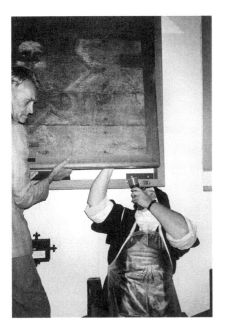

Dr Eugenia Nirowski examines the Templecombe Panel. (Courtesy of Rex Morgan)

Along with archaeologist Dr Eugenia Nitowski, archivist Audrey Dymock Herdsman, and other interested parties, Rex set about undertaking a thorough study of the panel, which the Church authorities allowed him to conduct by removing the panel from behind its glass casing.

When looking at a photograph of the panel, taken not long after it's discovery, Rex noted a 'nib' or hinge on the top right-hand corner of the panel, which had subsequently been sawn off when it had been placed as a 'picture' in the church. Also, the top plank of the panelled image was missing, and had been replaced to complete the 'picture', but gave a somewhat different view as to the likely identity of the original use of the object. Rex commented that it would be unlikely for an artist to have used five heavy boards as a background for a painting. He observes, 'If it were merely a decorative picture intended for horizontal suspension in order to be viewed, it seems highly unlikely that the artist would have chosen as his medium a massive panel of five long, thick and heavy boards'. He and Audrey Dymock believed there were originally *two* hinges atop the panel, and there is also evidence of lock marks; the conclusion, therefore, was that the so-called 'panel painting' was in fact the lid of a large box. In fact more than just a box, the proposal was that it was a box which had once contained the Shroud. Rex suggested that the box may have contained a reliquary (or perhaps *the* golden reliquary/Grail) with the Shroud inside, the dimensions of the box appear to suggest this, or it may have just held the cloth itself, folded, as it was during it's time in Constantinople, 'doubled in four'.

In 1989, Dr Eugenia Nitowski, a biblical archaeologist, was able to take samples of dust particles from the back of the panel and from the gaps between the planks. This procedure was conducted in front of three witnesses, and Rex filmed the proceedings. The results that followed were very interesting: 'Subsequent microscopic study and microphotographs by Nitowski of the samples has revealed a wide range of residual materials such as cotton, flax, pollens, calcium, amber particles, myrrh, aloes and several others.' There was also an unknown blue fibre, which Nitowski commented was also present on the Shroud.[iii]

Nitowski, who examined and photographed the Shroud samples that were taken by the Shroud of Turin Research Project (STURP)[iv] team in 1978, commented that such was the similarity between the samples that she repeatedly thought she was looking at samples from the Shroud itself.

Rex and his son, Christopher, then set about reconstructing a box – based upon the evidence from the Templecombe Panel – and looking for a plausible theory as to when and how the Shroud came to Somerset, and why the panelled lid was hidden in the ceiling of Molly Drew's cottage.

When Could the Shroud have Come to Somerset?

There is in the Shroud's history, that period from 1307 when the Templars were arrested in Paris on 13th October, to about mid-1350s when there is almost no evidence, but much conflicting speculation, about the location of the Holy Shroud.

Rex Morgan

The reconstructed Templecombe Box lid. (Courtesy of Rex Morgan)

Having convincingly established his theory as to the purpose of the panel, the next thing for Rex Morgan to try and find out was if there was any evidence to suggest when, and if, it would have been possible for the Shroud to have come to England?

Ian Wilson has traced a very plausible and likely chronology of the whereabouts of the Shroud from the period when it was taken to Edessa in AD 50. Although it is known that the Shroud 'visited' other places on occasion for the privileged few to observe and venerate, it appears that from AD 50 it was held at Edessa until it was taken to Constantinople in 944. Historical documents tell us that it disappeared from Constantinople in 1204, and sometime after this date evidence suggests it was most likely acquired by the Knights Templar. Most Shroud scholars now agree that at some point in its history it was in the possession of the Knights.

The Templar's acquisition of the Shroud appears to coincide with the spread across Europe of what Vatican archivist Barbara Frale describes as the 'cult of the simulacra', which she identifies as a cult of copies of the face of the man on the Shroud, which were deemed to have special power:

> ... these simulacra started appearing in the (Templar) mansions of southern France, especially Provence; for some reason the cult there spread sooner and faster than anywhere else. The following decades witnessed a kind of explosion of copies, which meant that by the end of the thirteenth century they could be found in practically every country where the Templar was present.[v]

This appears to indicate that at this point in the thirteenth century, the Templars had a heightened awareness and knowledge of the Shroud. At about the same time, there was also a rapid transmission across Europe of the Grail stories.

From 1204 until its public appearance in Lirey in 1355, there have been many tantalising clues as to the whereabouts of the Shroud, which appears to have been in the possession of the Crusader leader and Burgundian Knight, Otho de la Roche, when he served as leader in Athens after the sack of Constantinople.

Compelling evidence now suggests that it was from la Roche that the Templars acquired the Shroud, and by the end of the thirteenth century they were almost certainly using it in their 'secret rites'.

On Friday, 13 October 1307, following persistent rumours that the Templars were worshipping an idol in the form of a bearded male head,

King Philip of France and the Pope seized this opportunity to attack the Templars, and in the early hours of the morning sealed orders were given for the arrest of all the Templars in France. Philip's henchmen were also instructed to seize the 'head or idol' and recover the fabled 'treasure' from the Paris preceptory. Nothing was ever found. Scholars disagree as to whether the Templars had been forewarned of the impending attack, but Morgan argues that it seems likely from the evidence known to us that they attempted to ensure that their most important treasures were removed from the country before the purge.

Two weeks before this calculated and unprovoked attack, the Templar fleet had sailed out of La Rochelle harbour to an unknown destination. Rex Morgan believes it was at this point that the Shroud came to England for safekeeping. From the English port of Poole, it is but a short journey to what would have been a quiet and unsuspected sanctuary for the Shroud. Made of oak, the Templecombe box was the container made for keeping Christianity's most sacred relic.

We may ask ourselves why did the Templars not give the Shroud into the possession of the Church? Well, it seems that as there were dubious circumstances attached to their acquisition of the Shroud, and as they believed that their sole *raison d'etre* was the service of Christ, it seems likely that they wanted to keep this priceless treasure for themselves. As they were only answerable to the Pope, they would have known that if he demanded it, they would have to give it up. That is why it had to be kept such a great secret. Some authorities suggest that, in fact, the Templars had a plan to establish an alternative Church, to be known as the Temple.

As was mentioned in an earlier chapter, there were notable families across Europe whose task was the responsibility for the safekeeping of the Shroud. They often had family members who were Templars, or who had close connections with the Templars. Rex Morgan believes:

It seems indisputable that the de Charny family had a great deal to do with the Shroud, and it seems equally likely that if they had possession of it during the difficult period of the twelve and thirteen hundreds, as many scholars assert, and since they and other families associated with the Shroud throughout that time were also closely associated with the Order of the Temple, it is quite plausible to assume that they would have collaborated with the knights to conceal their possession from those who sought to obtain it.

Outhouse or Ritual Chapel?

Certainly, Rex Morgan's theory as to the true purpose of the panel, and his suggestion as to when exactly this may have happened, seems a very plausible one. As to his theory of when and how it came to be in the ceiling of Molly Drew's cottage, he suggests that when the Templars were suppressed in England, which was a few years after the suppression in France, that the Shroud was again taken from the box. The lid, with it's image of a head – which he describes as 'a damning piece of evidence' – was removed from the base of the box, and, as it had been in contact with the Sacred object, it was secreted away into the ceiling of the Priest's House, and covered with plaster. He surmises:

> If my theory of the construction of the box is correct then the simplest way to disengage the lid from the box itself, particularly if done in haste, would be to cut off one of the wooden nibs (the missing left-hand one) and draw the lid sideways from the rod connecting it to the other nib, hence the absence of one of the nibs and the existence of the other. The lid, now simply a panel bearing a portrait, was then concealed in the ceiling of the chaplain's house.[vi]

What of the room where the panel was found hidden in 1944? This room, which is often wrongly termed as an outhouse, was part of the cottage in which Mrs Drew lived (one of a terrace of three). This room, as mentioned before, was at a lower level than the cottage – 'a step down', said Mrs Drew. It could have held about ten people. It had no window, only a small circular stone 'porthole' which survived until modern times, and which the author has reason to believe is still in existence today, in the hands of a local collector.[vii]

If Audrey Dymock Herdsman's hypothesis is correct – that West Court Cottages were originally the Templar chaplain's house – it could be that the Knights were using the room for some form of ritual or ceremony. Morgan suggests that as the Templars were frequently noted for performing ceremonies involving an image of the head of Christ, then the outhouse could have been a symbolic representation of Jesus's tomb, similar, he suggests, to 'the ritual of Freemasons'.

We know that the Templars in England were not dealt with as harshly as their French brethren. No torture was used to extract confessions, and none were put to death; though the last Grand Master, William De la More, died in prison. After the Order was dissolved, many knights re-joined existing monastic orders, but many more simply 'disappeared' into the secular community. The Templecombe preceptory passed to the Crown in 1312[viii] and by 1338/9 it had become the property of the Hospitallers, where it was described as the ninth wealthiest Hospitaller House in England.[ix]

The 'outhouse' was demolished in recent times, taking with it any remaining evidence as to it's true purpose, although Morgan suggests that even now there may still be some archaeological evidence remaining hidden under the ground, but that is for the future.

It is greatly to be hoped that the singular importance of the nature of Molly Drews discovery; of the panel painting itself; and of the village of Templecombe in this continuing and great mystery of the Holy Shroud and of the Templars and of the Holy Grail, will be properly appreciated in the future and that further study and opinion may one day prove or disprove my speculation that the Shroud was once in England.

Rex Morgan, 1987

ENDNOTES

i Excerpt from a lecture given by Rex Morgan at the International Scientific Symposium in Nice in 1997. Paper entitled 'Did the Shroud Come to England?'

ii Faith, J., *The Knights Templar in Somerset*, p.26. (The History Press, 2009)

iii Nitowski, Dr E., Templecombe Samples Catalogue (1995)

iv STURP: The Shroud of Turin Research Project, a major study of the Turin Shroud conducted by a team of international scientists in 1978

v Frale, B., *The Templars and the Shroud of Christ*, p.23, p.232 (Maverick, 2011)

vi Morgan, Rex, paper entitled 'Did the Shroud Come to England?'

vii Faith, J., *The Knights Templar in Somerset*, p.35. (The History Press, 2009)

viii *Victoria County History II*, p.147; Cal Mem Rolls 326-7, p.347

ix 'Knights Hospitaller in England', pp.183-6 (Camden Society, 1857)

6

THE TEMPLARS, THE IDOL AND THE GRAIL

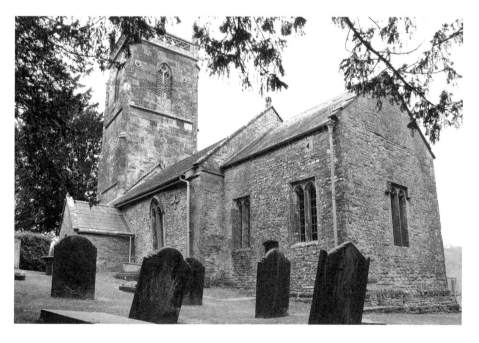

Cameley Church, Somerset. (Courtesy of Alex Meadows)

For the first time in history, a window opens upon the inaccessible future. An all important question arises here, which better not be answered by the Cheshire Cat, but by the rest of us...

Through the Turin Shroud ...
The extraordinary blueprint ...
The only window on the future in the cosmos, on the cosmos.[i]

Dame Isabel Piczek, particle physicist

An Idol in the Form of a Head

There has been endless debate amongst scholars as to the identity of the mysterious 'idol' in the form of a head, venerated by the Knights Templar. The 'idol' played a key part in the accusations of heresy, which were levelled against them by King Philip (the fair) of France, and the Pope, and ultimately brought about the suppression of the Order. Many descriptions of the 'idol' were given at the trials of the Templars; nearly all amount to what was probably the same object, a bearded male head, sometimes described as 'on cloth' or 'carved out of wood' or 'painted on a panel'. Here we are probably dealing with an original item, and various 'copies' of it, executed in different mediums.

For example, William of Arreblay, the Preceptor of Soisons, described the 'idol' thus: 'It seemed to have two faces and a terrible countenance, and a silver beard'.[ii] This could certainly be a valid description of the Shroud, as opened to it's full length one can clearly see the 'two heads', which are in fact the front and back of the same head. Yet another Templar, Hugh de Pairaud, described it as having 'four feet, two at the front part of the face, and two at the back.'[iii] Again, this is exactly how the folded Shroud could be described. One must remember that whilst these confessions were being extracted, the Knights were suffering from the agonies of the most appalling torture techniques, including having their feet roasted over a fire, and other such horrors.

Today, most Shroud scholars acknowledge that at some point in its history the Shroud was known about, and probably guarded by, the Templars, who venerated it as their most sacred relic.

This, it has been concluded, is probably the clue to the origins of the strange stories concerning mysterious secret ceremonies performed by the Knights. From what we know, these ceremonies were usually performed after dark, in secret places often with a guard at the door, and attended only by the highest members of the Order.

Rumour and speculation was rife concerning what happened during these secret meetings, and by the time of the arrest of the Templars in France on 13 October 1307, the Knights were accused of being involved in various forms of malpractice, which included sodomy, devil worship, denying Christ, and the reverence of an 'idol' in the form of a disembodied, bearded male head.

Many theories have been put forward as to the validity of these accusations and what lay behind them, and why the Knights who were arrested were prepared to face death rather than reveal the identity of the 'idol' that they revered?

Whether they had purchased the Shroud after the sack of Constantinople, or been chosen as guardians of it, what is very evident is that they did not want it to fall into anyone else's hands. The Templars understood the Shroud to be the most sacred relic on Earth. It provided physical proof of Jesus's Passion, death and resurrection. The Shroud held the key to the eternal life of the Spirit, and was thought to be an antidote for the evils of the world. The Shroud was the validation that Jesus Christ was all he had claimed to be, and hope for the future of mankind. As such, it must be protected and preserved at any cost. The Templars had become the guardians of the Grail.

Evidence given at the trials seems to suggest that it was only the highest dignitaries of the Order who had been allowed sight of the Shroud, or were even aware of it. However, at the very same time that the Grail legends were sweeping across Europe, another phenomenon was emerging which would have been accessible to lesser members of the Order and perhaps to others in the community as well. This cult was something that Vatican historian Barbara Frale calls the 'cult of the simulacra'.

A simulacrum is an image, traditionally the likeness of a god, which was of great importance in its own right, and was thought to have special power. The simulacra were, Frale suggests, copies of the face on the Shroud, 'disembodied' as it would have appeared to observers of the Constantinople reliquary. These simulacra, she observes, were either carved in bas-relief or painted on wood. She also believes that they could be found in nearly every country where there was a Templar presence, and she suggests that the cult arrived in England via the Templar Master, Roncelin de Fos.[iv]

The idea of an image of a disembodied man's face being revered by the Templars has been borne out by other commentators; some suggest that every Templar preceptory possessed a copy of this face, which was probably the origin of the infamous 'idol'. Certainly this would account for the various descriptions of the head, which, as Malcolm Barber points out, had been seen 'as far apart as Paris and Limassol', and was described as variously being 'painted on a beam, was made of wood, silver and gold leaf, and had four legs, two at the front, and two at the back'.[v]

What happened to these simulacra after the suppression of the Templars? It would seem hard to believe that they were all destroyed, particularly as it

The Cameley head. (Courtesy of Alex Meadows)

appears there would have been very many of them. Much more likely is that they were hidden away by Templar sympathizer's, or others who knew their real identity as copies of the face on the Shroud.

In Somerset there are two mysterious heads which could both be contenders for such 'simulacra'; one is the Templecombe Panel, which was found at Templecombe in Somerset, and the other currently resides at Cameley church, Templecloud – another important Templar location.

The wooden Cameley head is carved in bas-relief, and is examined in detail in my previous book *The Knights Templar in Somerset*. We know that the Templecombe Panel was concealed within a ceiling for possibly hundreds of years until its discovery during the Second World War. The Cameley head has an equally interesting history: not mentioned in the church guide, it appears to have been moved in and out of the church, and in the guardianship of various local people, before it came to its present resting place, gazing down from the church tower and looking for all the world like the guardian of the place.

After several years, and several attempts by certain people to try and have the Cameley head scientifically identified and dated, nothing, as far as we know, has been resolved.

The Grail in Somerset

Could it be that at some time in its long and mysterious history the Shroud once came to the South West? Certainly, there seems to be indications that *something* believed to be the burial cloth of Christ was once at Glastonbury, and suggestions that fragments of it may have survived until modern times, indeed it is possible that these fragments may *still* survive somewhere locally today. There are compelling links between Joseph of Arimathea and both the Shroud and blood of Christ, links that take us back to the time of Jesus's crucifixion.

There is documentary evidence in the form of the fifth-century parchment found in Georgia, which recounts Joseph collecting the blood of Christ on two cloths, a shroud and a facecloth. There are two cloths – surviving to this day – that scientists have discovered are soaked in the blood of the same individual, indicating that both covered the same body at almost the same time. Both have ancient and mysterious origins, one is known as the Sudarium of Oviedo, the other as the Shroud of Turin. There is a possibility that these are the very same cloths chronicled in the Georgian manuscript. The Eastern Orthodox Church still conducts services that centre on the *Epitaphios*, a cloth bearing the image of the crucified Christ.

In later times, legend recounts that Joseph was the original founder of the Church at Glastonbury. We must consider as a possibility the idea that either Joseph himself or another early apostle came to Glastonbury, bringing with him the Shroud as evidence of the miracle of the resurrection, and the inspiration behind the founding of the early Church in these parts. There is also the eighth-/ninth-century 'Book of Armagh', which tells of St Patrick bringing the blood of Christ, in a linen cloth, to Glastonbury.

Glastonbury is certainly traditionally believed to have links with the Irish Celtic Church. It is thought that St Patrick founded an early church on the site of the Old Church at Glastonbury Abbey. This same church was venerated as a relic itself during the reign of Henry de Blois, Abbot of Glastonbury and Bishop of Winchester.

As brother of the King of England, Henry de Blois had close connections with the line of families who were guardians of the Shroud, a line which culminated in the Savoy family, who had a chapel built at Turin Cathedral to house the Shroud, where it resides to this day, although the guardianship of the relic now belongs to the Catholic Church.

Undoubtedly Henry had knowledge of the Shroud, and it is highly likely that the Chapel of the Holy Sepulchre at Winchester Cathedral was used during his bishopric for services that were similar to those conducted today in the Eastern Orthodox Church, in the form of the Good Friday Liturgy. We may speculate that a chapel with a similar function once existed at Glastonbury. Documentary evidence tells us of a special play that was written just before Henry's reign for performance at Glastonbury; this play featured the miraculous Shroud of Christ.

What of the anonymous author of *Perlesvaus*, who tells us that Perceval's sister, Dindrane, cut fragments of the shroud held in the Perilis Chapel at Glastonbury? The Shroud was once reputed to have been kept at Glastonbury in the Perilis Chapel, could this Perilis Chapel have been the ancient Chapel on Beckery Island, close to the Perilis bridge and Wearyall Hill? A chapel surrounded by marshland would certainly have been a safe place to house such a precious relic.

This idea is also reminiscent of the legend of fragments of the Shroud reputedly housed at the old chapel at Lamanna. Did each location have fragments of this precious cloth that had once been brought to the South West in its entirety?

Certainly, both places claimed to have very early Christian foundations, and both laid claim to the story of Joseph of Arimathea visiting, some say with the boy Jesus. Is it possible that in reality these are both remnants of a long-lost oral tradition which recounted the Shroud, with its miraculous image of Christ, once having been brought to the South West?

By the twelfth and thirteenth centuries, as the Grail legends spread throughout Christendom, and the heroes were King Arthur and his knights, the Shroud was to be found in the guise of the Holy Grail, the mysterious object with transforming qualities, which could bring about healing and eternal life ...

Had this very Shroud of Jesus – the Holy Grail – once resided in the South West of England? Could this be the very reason that Glastonbury was believed to have been the 'holyest erthe in England'? It may be that the Shroud was brought here at the dawn of Christianity, or perhaps it was brought here by the Knights Templar after their arrest in France in the thirteenth century and housed at Templecombe, as Rex Morgan suggests. On the other hand, we are faced with the possibility that it has resided in England twice in its history.

Somehow, in a very special way, Glastonbury and its environs became imbued with a sacred mystery that remains to this day, sleeping beneath the layers of modernity. The Shroud, like the Grail, has proved an enigma ever since the earliest knowledge of its existence. Both are objects that contain the sacred blood of Jesus; each were historically only revealed to a few select people, in secretive and mysterious ceremonies; each claimed to have special transforming and healing properties. Both were considered so sacred that people were prepared to sacrifice their own lives rather than give the object into the hands of those who were unworthy; the distinction of each blurs. Both Shroud and Grail present a key to a different understanding of reality. As Jesus himself said, 'The Kingdom of Heaven is all around you, but you cannot see it.'

Today, if we open our minds and hearts, we are faced with the possibility, as Isabel Piczeck suggests, that the Shroud is the 'blueprint' for the universe; or in the words of Dr Andrew Silverman, 'Perhaps 2,000 years ago Jesus deliberately left us a clue which he knew would be unraveled by science.'[vi]

The Light. (Courtesy of Henry Rothwell)

ENDNOTES

i Piczeck, I., *Alice in Wonderland and the Shroud of Turin* (1996)
ii Barber, M., *The Trial of the Templars*, p.185 (Cambridge, 1978)
iii *Ibid*. p.83.
iv Frale, B., *The Templars and the Shroud of Christ*, p.232-3
v Barber, M., *The Trial of the Templars*, p.76 (Cambridge, 1978)
vi Silverman, Dr A., *The Light that Shone in the Darkness* (www.lightoftheshroud.com)

APPENDIX

JOSEPH OF ARIMATHEA: MYSTERY MAN OF THE GOSPELS

A Paper by Ed Prior

Joseph of Arimathea. All Christians and many non-Christians know his name and the crucial role the Gospels tell us he played in taking the body of Jesus from the Cross and placing it in a tomb. But we know almost nothing about who he really was and what he did after the Christian event known as the 'Resurrection of Jesus'. There is only one short paragraph about Joseph in each of the canonical Gospels and not a word about his activities in Luke's Acts of the Apostles. Of all the characters in the Gospels other than Jesus, few played a more important role in early Christianity than Joseph of Arimathea – and yet he is arguably its biggest mystery.

Joseph of Arimathea does appear in several non-canonical Christian documents. European legends suggest that he (and others) left Judea to escape the wrath of High Priest Caiaphas for his role in the disappearance of Jesus, and crossed the Mediterranean with a handful of other Jewish refugees to land in either southern France or through the Strait of Gibraltar to south-western Britain. For reasons we shall discuss, it is fashionable among today's biblical scholars to dismiss any notion that Joseph ever left Judea – and some even dispute his very existence. Joseph has also gained recognition because of the Shroud of Turin, an ancient linen cloth imprinted with the mysterious image of a crucified male purported to be Jesus. If it is eventually proven to be legitimate, it would have originally belonged to Joseph – who, the Gospels tell us, wrapped the body of Jesus in a linen cloth before burial.

In this chapter we will examine what little is known about Joseph of Arimathea; why does his name vanish after the Resurrection event, as do the names of Lazarus, Mary Magdalene, and others? Did Caiaphas arrest Joseph for suspicion of removing Jesus's body from the tomb, as the apocryphal 'Gospel of Nicodemus' suggests? Or did Joseph escape Judea and head for Europe and finally south-western Britain, as legends and some disputed medieval documents state? Is there any ancient written or archaeological evidence for this? How did Joseph come to be associated with the legendary Holy Grail in British lore and history? Many have asked the same question as historian Geoffrey Ashe, 'Why Joseph?'[i] Did the European legends evolve because of confusion by early Vatican scribes and historians between the name of 'Britain' and the name of the 'Britium' fortress in ancient Edessa?

We will examine the non-canonical as well as the canonical Christian literature; following Thomas Jefferson's advice[ii] to 'Read all the histories of Christ, as well as those whom a council of ecclesiastics have decided for us …' It is believed that many accounts of Jesus's life were rejected as canon because they were regarded as supplementary rather than false[iii]. Two of these are particularly important for this review: the 'Lost Gospel of Peter' and the 'Gospel of Nicodemus'.

Did Joseph of Arimathea Really Exist?

Skeptics[iv] suspect Joseph was 'invented' by Gospel writers so that Jesus fulfilled the Isaiah 53:9 biblical belief that the Jewish Messiah would 'make his grave with the wicked, and the rich in his death … ' The 'wicked' would obviously be the two criminals crucified on either side of Jesus, according to the Gospels; Joseph of Arimathea would be 'the rich'. Other skeptics point out that there is no town in present-day Israel or Jordan with the name 'Arimathea', but the Muslims renamed virtually every Judean city after their AD 638 conquest of the Holy Land. Dr Dan Bahat, the former Chief Archaeologist of Jerusalem, suspects[v] that the original Arimathea was located at the Arab village today named 'er-Ram'. There are other candidates for the location, including near Lydda, where, from the fifth to eighth century, documents[vi] indicate Joseph might have helped found a church; the Arab cities of Ramatayim and Ramalla are also possibilities.

Biblical scholar John Dominic Crossan's grisly suspicion is that Jesus's body was consumed on the Cross[vii] by vultures and/or wild dogs. If this were the case, there would obviously be no role for Joseph of Arimathea to take down Jesus's body from the Cross (Crossan is also a member of the so-called Jesus Seminar[viii], which disputes eighty per cent of Gospel stories). Yet another possibility is that Jesus's body was buried by the Romans in a common grave pit with crucified thieves[ix]. The problem with all these theories is that they fly in the face of strong Christian written traditions, primarily in the Gospels, that Jesus's body was indeed entombed – and the tomb was visited by several Apostles and women followers who verified that his body had mysteriously vanished. If, as seems likely, a tomb was employed for Jesus, *someone* had to be responsible for placing his body there; the Gospels make clear that his Apostles (except for the unidentified 'Beloved Disciple') were cowering in fear during his burial. The Gospels unanimously report (Matt 27:57; Mark 15:43; Luke 23:50; John 19:38) that a rich merchant named Joseph of Arimathea took on this critical task. While it may never be proven to the satisfaction of the doubters, we conclude it is probable that Joseph of Arimathea was a real person and played a key role in the start of the Christian faith.

Was the tomb Joseph's? Only Matthew 27:60 states Jesus's body was placed in Joseph's 'own unused tomb'. Yet neither John 19:42 nor Mark 15:46, nor the detail-oriented Luke 23:53 confirm that the tomb belonged to Joseph, an omission difficult to explain if it did. However, the non-canonical 'Lost Gospel of Peter 6:3' states that Joseph brought Jesus to his 'own tomb, called the Garden of Joseph'. Since the name 'Joseph' was one of the most popular in ancient Judea, it is possible that the garden was named for another Joseph – not the one from Arimathea. It also seems unlikely that a garden in the Jerusalem cemetery near Mount Olive would be named for someone from Arimathea. The notion that the tomb was Joseph's should be regarded as possible but not probable.

Since virtually all of our information about Jesus and Joseph comes from the Gospels, it is important to be aware of their shortcomings. The Gospels were established as Christian Canon at the Councils of Hippo and of Carthage around AD 400; four gospels were selected and dozens of others rejected and many destroyed. Why only four? Church father Irenaeus believed, 'There are four winds ... therefore there should be four gospels.'[x] We may never know how much valuable information about Jesus, Joseph and others was lost from these so-called 'apocryphal gospels' because this view eventually became accepted. Unfortunately, there is also much evidence that the early Christian transcribers of the Gospels made well-meaning changes to the original text of Mark, Matthew and other gospel writers – sadly, we do not have the 'original' gospels[xi]. All this adds to the challenge of solving the mysteries of Joseph of Arimathea. Let's examine one of the intriguing non-canonical documents concerning this man. Since he is the only person with that name we will discuss, for the rest of the chapter 'Joseph' refers to 'Joseph of Arimathea'.

There are many legends that Joseph was an uncle of Jesus. Pilate's decision to release Jesus's body to Joseph is often cited as proof of a family tie between the two, but Roman law gave Pilate the authority to make a local decision on such requests regardless of family considerations[xii]. The medieval 'Harleian Manuscript' collection (asis.com/~stag/royalty.html) in the British Library includes a family tree for Joseph which shows British kings as his descendants, names his wife (Enygeus) and states he was Jesus's uncle. But the Gospels and Acts are very thorough in stating who is related to whom; we know that Jesus's dozen Apostles included at least three pairs of brothers, Jesus and John the Baptist were cousins, Jesus's brother James became the leader of the faith until his murder, etc. Why would the Gospels neglect mentioning that Joseph was Jesus's uncle? Although such a family tie is possible, this question should have no impact on our goal of understanding Joseph's ultimate fate.

Why Would Joseph of Arimathea and Others Leave Judea?

To examine the legends that Joseph went to Britain, we first have to ask if there are any valid reasons to believe that he really left his Judean homeland. The 'Gospel of Nicodemus' states that Caiaphas had Joseph arrested and imprisoned[xiii] after Jesus's disappearance – yet there is no mention of such an arrest in Luke's 'Acts of the Apostles'. So could it have really happened? We know that both Caiaphas and the Romans were angry when Jesus vanished from the tomb and his followers proclaimed he had risen from the dead. A Roman decree authorized by the Emperor was issued[xiv] sometime between 50 BC to AD 50 that stated: 'The Decree on Grave Robbery, ordinance of Caesar: If anyone extracts the buried, I order a trial … the offender to be sentenced to capital punishment for Violation of Sepulture.' Determining a more exact date for the decree is difficult, but it may have been issued in response to the disappearance of Jesus's body – and Jews knew that if the Romans accused them of such an act in a trial, it meant automatic execution by crucifixion. Caiaphas, of course, was furious. He had been trying to minimize any anti-Roman reactions by his people to Jesus's preaching; the High Priests all had a relatively luxurious lifestyle[xv] under Roman rule, as long as they could keep order among the citizens of Jerusalem. But when Jesus vanished from his tomb and his followers proclaimed his resurrection, the Acts tell us that Jesus's popularity exploded – and Caiaphas would have known of Joseph's public and key role in placing Jesus's body in a tomb. The earlier apparent 'resurrection' of Lazarus that Jesus had presided over had also gained him many Jewish converts (John 12:11); the revenge planned by the High Priests was stated bluntly in John 12:10: '... the Chief Priests consulted that they might put Lazarus also to death ... ' If Caiaphas was this angry at Lazarus for his role in gaining Jewish converts to Jesus's cause, imagine his reaction to Joseph's role in placing Jesus's body into a tomb – where Caiaphas believed it could easily be stealthily removed by disciples – rather than simply placing the body into the traditional[xvi] Jewish 'trench grave' 5 to 7 feet underground, where most average citizens were interred. John 19:38 tells us that Joseph had 'fear of the Jews'– meaning the High Priests.

Caiaphas had no doubt that some of Jesus's disciples had secretly removed the body (Matthew 28:13); who would have been on his list of suspects? Certainly the *last* persons at the tomb before Jesus vanished – and the *first* persons to report that he was missing. According to the Gospels, Joseph and Nicodemus (mentioned only in John) were the last at the tomb. Even some modern scholars suspect Joseph[xvii] of involvement in Jesus's disappearance, so it would not be surprising if Caiaphas did as well. The Gospels further tell us that the first to discover the empty tomb were all women: the 'Three Mary's'[xviii] (Mary Magdalene – who some believe was the sister of Lazarus; Mary Salome; and Mary Cleopas) and several other women, with each Gospel differing slightly as to names. Some scholars today suspect the women[xix] in the disappearance of Jesus's body. They may well have had strong reasons to fear Caiaphas' anger. They would all know that – as women – they had no defenses in a Jewish court if Caiaphas accused them of removing Jesus's body. 'Men owned women's reproductive capacities; treated as chattels, confined to home, not even allowed to testify in Jewish courts'[xx]. They surely knew that, like Joseph and Lazarus, their lives could be in mortal danger if they stayed in Judea – not only from Caiaphas, but also the Romans.

Pilate, always interested in impressing his superiors in Rome, was called 'cruel and bloodthirsty' by Agrippa, grandson of Jewish King Herod the Great, and would have pursued anyone suspected of involvement in Jesus's disappearance. It should be clear that, while all the Apostles feared Caiaphas, Lazarus, the Three Mary's, and certainly Joseph were in special danger for their lives due to their association with either Jesus' apparent resurrection, or the disappearance of Jesus – both events assumed by Caiaphas to be outrageous hoaxes, according to the Gospels.

Could all five have decided to flee Judea and sail to Europe, as some ancient books and legends suggest? Doubters point to von Dobschuetz's[xxi] reference to a seventh-century Syrian-Nestorian document stating that Joseph's grave was discovered in 605 in Jerusalem. According to the document, Judeans dug for treasure – after getting Muslim permission – and found a sarcophagus inscribed, 'This is the sarcophagus of the councilor Joseph, who gave a tomb for the body of Jesus'. It would have been unusual for Joseph's family to forgo the traditional use of a small box called an ossuary in which to place his bones after his corpse had decayed, but it is certainly possible. We cannot be sure of the authenticity of the fifth- to eighth-century legends mentioned earlier that Joseph and others built a church in Lydda, and we have the same doubts about the seventh-century Syrian-Nestorian document. We conclude that it is certainly possible that Joseph and a number of Jesus's disciples could have fled Jerusalem because of fear of Caiaphas and Pilate. If so, they could have traveled to any of the many areas in Europe where there were strong and friendly Jewish enclaves that resulted from the Diaspora when Jews fled Judea because of repeated invasions.

Joseph and Company to Europe?

There are several documents of disputed age that tell a story of Christian disciples, both men and women, who board a ship along the Judean coast and land on the shores of southern Europe. There is no way to verify these tales, and even their authorship is questionable – with one exception. One of these, written around 1600, is authored by the Curator of the Vatican Library: Cardinal Baronius. Unfortunately, he does not reference his source or sources for the story. He wrote that Joseph of Arimathea, the Three Mary's, Lazarus and some other disciples took a ship from the coast of Israel and sailed to southern France in AD 35[xxii]. The timing, according to Baronius' story, is intriguing, since the first Christian martyr (Stephen) was murdered around AD 35 and the fear of the High Priests among the followers of Jesus would have been at a fever pitch at that time. There is a local tradition[xxiii] in Arles that the first Jewish settlers came to that part of France in a boat. Even today, the French celebrate the legendary presence of Magdalene and others there with parades and exhibitions[xxiv], some even displaying her alleged skull! It seems unlikely that a Cardinal – especially the Pope's Vatican Curator – would have simply made up this story. It is possible he based his tale on European legends, but we may never know for certain.

Another far older document, the *Recognitions* by Clement (assumed to be the early Pope who knew Peter, but this is not certain), is believed to be from the first or second century and relates a tale of a caravan of disciples led by a preaching Peter; they walked up the Judean coastline all the way to Antioch. S.A. Harvey, in the *Cambridge History of Christianity* (p. 351), wrote, 'Paul's letter to the Galatians and further statements from Acts present Antioch as the base from which the first Christians launched their missions out into the larger Mediterranean.' According to Clement, the caravan included Lazarus, Joseph, and unnamed Christian 'women' – probably including the Three Mary's. But Clement does *not* state that they left on a ship.

The Golden Legend, written around 1264 by Jacob of Voragine, and the *Life of Magdalene*, written in either the ninth, tenth, or eleventh century, with the name of its author still debated, both tell stories of disciples travelling to Europe by ship and settling there. In none of the four accounts – *Baronius, Recognitions, The Golden Legend*, or the *Life of Magdalene* – are the lists of names exactly consistent with each other. However, Lazarus, Joseph of Arimathea, and the Three Mary's appear to be the only five who are in all four accounts. Of course, this does not prove they all left Judea. But the fact is that after the disappearance of Jesus from the tomb, we never again read about Lazarus, or about the Three Mary's, or about Joseph in the Acts of the Apostles or *any* of the canonical Christian literature. Despite the key roles each had at the founding of the Christian faith – they all simply vanish.

In three of the four accounts of a group of Jesus's followers leaving Judea for Europe, we find the name of Martha, the sister of Lazarus. Why would she leave, since she had not been at Jesus's tomb after his disappearance and was under no threat from Caiaphas? The answer could be that it would have been sensible for her to leave Judea for Europe with her two family members – Lazarus and Mary – rather than remain as a woman alone in male-dominated Judea at the home she shared with them. There are several other strong hints in the Gospels that these five – Joseph, the Three Mary's, and Lazarus – may have left Judea, along with others.

These hints are in the names that *are* included in the Gospels – and those name that are *not*. For example, the authors of the four gospels deliberately did not include their own names. We attribute the Gospels to men named Mark, Matthew, Luke and John based on traditions and speculations, but we cannot be certain who these authors really were[xxv]. The reason for the secrecy may be remarkably simple: fear of the Romans and fear of the

Jewish High Priests. If they had known the names of the Gospel writers, the authors and their families could have been in significant danger. The same fear could also explain the mysterious abrupt ending of Mark's gospel. The earliest version ends with Mark 16:8, after the women find Jesus's tomb empty: 'And they went out quickly, and fled from the sepulcher for they trembled and were amazed; neither said they anything to any man for they were afraid.' Of course, this cannot be correct; we know from John's gospel that the women told the Apostles that Jesus's body was missing and several of them ran to the tomb to see for themselves. Why does Mark not tell us this? The simplest explanation may be that Mark, author of the first gospel, knew the women were gone from Judea and safely in Europe – so he named them. But the two Apostles who ran to the tomb, according to John 20:3-10, were Peter and the 'Beloved Disciple' – possibly the Apostle John – who were probably both still alive at the time Mark or his earlier source wrote the gospel[xxvi]. Had Mark mentioned their presence at the tomb where Jesus disappeared, they both would have been in serious trouble with the High Priests and the Romans.

By the time Luke wrote his gospel, some years[xxvii] after Mark, Peter was now deceased and Luke, therefore, felt free to mention his presence at the tomb (Luke 24:12) – but since John was still alive (and may have lived into his nineties, according to Christian traditions), Luke protected him and did not mention his visit to the tomb. We also note that Nicodemus' role in helping Joseph place Jesus's body in the tomb is not mentioned at all in Mark, Matthew or Luke; Nicodemus appears only in John's gospel, where he is mentioned twice (John 3:1-21, 19:39). Why do Mark, Matthew and Luke fail to mention Nicodemus?

They were probably protecting him because there is evidence Nicodemus remained in Jerusalem. The Gospel of Nicodemus indicates that Nicodemus had a home in Jerusalem and there are Jewish records that he and/ or his offspring were still living there as late as AD 69[xxviii]. It appears that Nicodemus may have successfully kept his role in the entombment of Jesus a closely guarded secret between himself and Joseph and some of the Apostles. Nicodemus probably remained a member in good standing of the Sanhedrin; he was not arrested after Jesus's body disappeared – only Joseph was, at least according to the Gospel of Nicodemus.

If this theory is correct, it not only explains the omission by gospel writers of the names of those disciples who remained in danger from the High Priests and the Romans; it also explains why Joseph's key role in the entombment of Jesus is revealed so prominently by all four gospel writers and even by the writer of the apocryphal 'Gospel of Peter'. They did not have to protect Joseph because they knew he, like Lazarus and the women who discovered the empty tomb, was gone from Judea and safe from the Jewish High Priests – and from Pilate and his Roman successors.

There are numerous legends about the route Joseph and his companions could have taken by ship to get to the European mainland[xxix]; J.W. Taylor[xxx] even sketches his best guess, from the Judean coast to Marseilles. Legends that the group was on a boat with no oars or rudder and drifted all the way to France[xxxi] are considered impossible because of the direction of currents in the Mediterranean[xxxii]. The main legends suggest that a group of Judean refugees landed on the southern shore of France. While many stayed in that region, according to these legends, Joseph and eleven companions split off from the group to migrate through France to its northern shore and then – either by boat or a land bridge that may have existed between Britain and the mainland 2,000 years ago – they journeyed to south-western Britain, and eventually Glastonbury, where they supposedly constructed several crude 'wattle and daub' huts for living and praying[xxxiii]. If Joseph was really worried that the Romans would be after him for his alleged role in moving Jesus's body from the tomb, such a move would have been sensible; the Romans had conquered most of Europe, but they would not invade Britain until AD 43 – so Joseph would have been safe if the Baronius date for the trip of AD 35 were valid. Even after Rome finally invaded, Pryor[xxxiv] notes '... most of Cornwall was hardly affected by the Roman conquest at all.' Unfortunately, that was not the case for the rest of Britain, much of which was invaded during many Roman military campaigns.

We know from the Acts 11:19-20 that the disciples began to spread the word of the new faith to Jews only, at least at first. Matthew 10:5-6 states: 'The twelve Jesus sent forth and commanded them, saying go not into the way of the Gentiles, and the Samaritans but go rather to the lost sheep of the house of Israel.' As the influence of Paul and others grew, this eventually changed and Gentiles also were targeted by later missionaries. Dr Doron Mendels of Hebrew University[xxxv] maps the spread of Jews across Europe, Asia and Africa after the Diaspora, and their dispersion following invasions and wars. The map shows a large bloc of Jews had spread into southern Europe – they were obvious candidates for proselytizing by the early Christian missionaries; however, there is no major Jewish bloc indicated anywhere in northern France or Gaul. Yet, Mendels' map suggests there was a Jewish bloc across the English Channel in south-western Britain. These Jews did not simply cross over the Channel from Jewish communities in northern France – because there weren't any there. Such a southern British Jewish enclave could certainly have been targeted for early Christian missionary activity. There is evidence that such an enclave existed. It may have been called 'Marazion'[xxxvi]; early Jewish immigrants were called 'Saracens', and many could have worked in the Cornwall tin mines, where phrases such as 'Jews' houses', 'Jews' tin,' 'Jews' works,' 'Bojewyan (abode of Jews),' and others may have been in common use[xxxvii]. Legends that Joseph was a tin merchant may have been strengthened by the proximity of the Cornwall tin mines to such a Jewish enclave[xxxviii]. Further legends that Joseph had often visited these mines and even brought his alleged nephew Jesus to 'walk upon England's Mountains Green' Jerusalem (William Blake, 1757-1827) were investigated by A.W. Smith. His article concluded ('The Legend of Christ's Visit to Britain', *Folklore*, vol. 100, No.1, 1989 pp. 63-83) that the evidence is 'weak' and the traditions are 'not demonstrably older than (the 1800s)'. We do know that by AD 314 there were at least three Christian British bishops – Restitutus (London), Eborius (York) and Adelphius, who went to the ecclesiastical council at Arles, France[xxxix]. This is a clear indication that Christianity had become well established in Britain by the early fourth century, and probably much sooner.

We shall next investigate documents from the early years of Christianity to see what insight we can gain about Joseph and his times.

Ancient Sources on the Spread of Christianity

In Luke's Acts of the Apostles 1:8, the resurrected Jesus tells his Apostles '... ye shall be witnesses unto me to the utmost part of the earth ... ' This is a clear order that they should preach the new Christian faith all the way to Britain, which would have been considered the 'utmost part of the earth' during that period. There are legends[XL] that Apostles such as Philip may have been in Britain; there was a significant flight of disciples out of Jerusalem to carry the words of Jesus to Europe and Asia, probably in part as a reaction to the horrifying murder of the first martyr, Stephen. Acts 11:19-20 states: '... those who scattered because of persecution after Stephen's murder travelled as far as Phoenicia, Cyprus and Antioch, speaking the word to none except Jews ... '. Second-century church father Irenaeus wrote[XLI] that there were 'churches founded in Spain and among the Celts', and Tertullian wrote[XLII] about the 'haunts of Britons, inaccessible to Romans but subjugated to Christ ... ' Had he seen the alleged lost second-century manuscript? Also the third-century church historian Hippolytus wrote[XLIII] that the disciple Aristobulus (mentioned in Romans 16:10) became a pastor in Britain. By the fourth century, St Hilary of Poitiers wrote[XLIV] 'The Apostles had built churches and the gospel had passed into Britain' and St John Chrysostom wrote[XLV] 'The British Isles ... have received the power of the word ... churches are there ... men everywhere discoursing matters in a different tongue but the same judgment ... ' A fifth-century Syriac document, according to W. Cureton (*Doctrine of the Apostles*, 1864, p. 34), stated:

> Rome and all Italy and Spain and Britain and Gaul ... received the Apostles' hand of priesthood from Simon Cephas, who went up from Antioch and became ruler and guide in the church. But the rest of the Apostles went to the distant countries of the Barbarians ...

Although these assorted ancient Christian writers make a case that some of Christ's Apostles may indeed have journeyed to Britain, none mention Joseph – an odd omission considering his alleged leading role in bringing Christianity to Britain. Gildas, one of the first English historians, wrote[XLVI] in the sixth century that, '... these Islands ... received the precepts of Christ ... in the last year, as we know, of the reign of Tiberius (37 AD, about the time disciples fled Jerusalem after Stephen's murder).' Curiously, again there is no mention of Joseph. There is another ancient source which we may be putting forward for the first time here in research into Joseph's fate – the *Toledoth Jesu*. This ancient Jewish source[XLVII] from the fourteenth century is possibly based on a document from the fifth or sixth century. This source obviously had no reason to cast a favorable light on the expansion of the Christian faith, but it states: 'The disciples [of Jesus] went out among the nations, three to the mountains of Ararat, three to Armenia, three to Rome, and three to the kingdoms by the sea.' In the first century, the 'three kingdoms by the sea' would have been referring to Spain, Gaul ... and Britain. If this odd document is truly based on information from the first century – and it is difficult to imagine why Jewish writers would have fabricated such a tale, since it demonstrates Christianity spreading all over Europe and Asia – it also implies that an early disciple of Jesus went to Britain.

No ancient non-medieval undisputed source has been found to date that specifically names Joseph as that disciple, which has reinforced the skepticism in academic circles that Joseph ever set foot in Britain. As we indicated earlier, the European legends that *have* sprung up suggest he brought the famous Holy Grail with him – the cup Jesus used at the Last Supper – have been greeted by most academic scholars as, at best, highly unlikely.

The von Harnack/Scavone Theory that Joseph Never Came to Britain: A Series of Clerical Errors

Oxford New Testament scholar Eric Eve wrote: 'The probability that the cup (the Grail) found its way to Joseph of Arimathea, and that both came here is nil, it is purely legendary.' Former Bishop of Edinburgh Richard Holloway calls it 'all good fun but absolute nonsense … there isn't any objective truth in any of it'. Of the possibility that Joseph came to Britain with the Holy Grail, historian Richard Barber (author of *The Holy Grail: Imagination and Belief*) concludes, 'It is pure literature'. (All the above quotes are from reference[XLVIII]).

Christian historian Adolf von Harnack believed, along with current Indiana University scholar Daniel Scavone, that there were a remarkable series of clerical errors that led to what was assumed to be evidence that Christianity had come to Britain early in the first century. We cannot comment on them in detail here, but will present an outline because of their importance. According to von Harnack[XLIX], a fifth- or sixth-century account in the Vatican *Liber Pontificalis* (a record of the Pope's correspondence) was in error; the account mentioned that a second-century 'King Lucius of Britain' had written to then-Pope Eleutherius and requested missionaries be sent to his country to help Christianize it. This story later found its way into the work of Bede, an eighth-century British historian, and its inclusion there contributed to its general acceptance as a historical fact. But von Harnack, assuming there were no British kings during that early period, noted there *was* a King Lucius Septimus Megas Abgar IX of Edessa, who had a fortress with the Latin name *Britium*. Von Harnack concluded the Vatican scribe who wrote the *Liber Pontificalis* item had mistaken the Edessan King Lucius of Britium for the apparently non-existent King Lucius of Britain!

Since an elaborate history appeared centuries later to describe King Lucius of Britain and the alleged missionaries sent by the Pope and their activities in Britain to begin a Christian church there, the entire prehistory of Christianity in Britain was now called into question by von Harnack – including whether or not Joseph had ever been there. The assumption that there were no British kings during the first and second centuries could be challenged by Tacitus' biography of his father-in-law, the Roman General Agricola[L], in which he wrote 'They [the British] were once ruled by kings, but are now divided under chieftains ... King Cogidumnus (one of several so-called 'British Client Kings') was a most faithful ally'. So the word 'king' was in use in early Britain, even if it did not mean King of the entire nation. Von Harnack believed there was no British King Lucius – but there is an independent tradition of a Christian British king named Lucius, who was displaced from Britain by the Roman Empire along with many other Britains and sent to the Raetia province (today in Switzerland) to help fight off the barbarians. This Lucius is supposedly buried in the Swiss Chur Cathedral. David J. Knight, in his book *King Lucius of Britain*[LI], includes evidence that the displacement of British tribes to Raetia happened near the time period when *Liber Pontificalis* had Lucius writing to the Pope. Nevertheless, the weight of today's academic opinion seems to strongly favour von Harnack's 'clerical error' theory.

Indiana University scholar Daniel Scavone[LII] also believes that mistakes may explain several aspects of the 'Joseph in Britain' legends; in Scavone's words, there were 'misunderstandings by which Joseph of Arimathea could be accepted by medieval writers as an apostle to Britain.'[LIII] As we discussed earlier, a major problem for those who believe Joseph did come there is to explain why there is no mention of him in early Christian writings or by the earliest British Christian historian Gildas in *De Excidio Britanniae* – particularly troublesome since Gildas would have had access to ancient records in cathedrals across the country, possibly including Glastonbury. How could he have not been aware that a major gospel figure like Joseph had allegedly founded the British Church?

The first serious and supposedly non-fictional association of Joseph with Britain would not occur until William of Malmesbury's revised *Enquiry into the Antiquity of the Church of Glastonbury* – published (with major revisions and additions by the monks of Glastonbury) in 1247. This doctored version of Malmesbury's 1125 original related a detailed story of Joseph of Arimathea coming with a dozen or so disciples to Glastonbury and founding the church there after St Philip, then supposedly stationed in Gaul. Malmesbury's original text from 1125 had only speculated that Philip might have been in Gaul – and had no mention of Joseph at all, even though Malmesbury had access to the Glastonbury library when he wrote his original. But he did write in that 1125 book that, 'Documents say Christ's disciples erected Glastonbury Church,' so he had some reference that he unfortunately did not list – before the controversial revisions by the Glastonbury monks to his original book over a century later.

Scavone theorizes[LIV] that even Malmesbury's speculation about Philip in Gaul was the result of a misunderstanding by Malmesbury of his source, a ninth-century Bishop – Freculphus – who had written that, '*Phillipus … Gallis praedicavit Christum*'. Scavone believes there was enough ambiguity in Freculphus' statement that Malmesbury believed he was referring to Philip preaching in Gaul, rather than preaching *among* the Gauls in Galatia, Turkey. Scavone goes further with this 'comedy of errors' theory by challenging the 1247 revised book's account of the '12 hides' (1 hide = 120 acres) given tax-free to Joseph and his colleagues to live and worship near Glastonbury by 'good King' Arvirargus (or Arviragus). Scavone and others noticed that the Roman satirist Juvenal had written a farce in which he used the line, 'You will capture some King – perhaps Arviragus will tumble out of his British wagon!' Scavone suspects British historian Geoffrey of Monmouth (in around 1136) decided to use this name from Juvenal's farce to name the British King from AD 44 to AD 54[LV]. The Glastonbury monks, in this theory, then used the name of King Arviragus as the man who gave Joseph and companions the tax-free hides in their 1247 revision of Malmesbury's 1125 account.

Since Geoffrey had spent seven pages extolling King Arviragus as a major enemy of the Roman invaders, it is difficult to understand why Geoffrey would have invented such adventures using a fake name from a Roman satirist – but that is Scavone's theory. For the twelve tax-free hides of land that Arviragus supposedly gave Joseph and his followers who arrived in Britain, the Domesday Book – housed in the London Public Record Office – has an intriguing citation. This book, commissioned in 1085 by King William I, states that the 'Home of God possesses in its own villa 12 hides of land which have never paid tax … the Abbey chapel contains the Secretum Domini (Secret of the Lord).' Why was the land given tax-free? What is the 'Secret of the Lord'? Could this be a clue that the Joseph legends are true? We may never know.

Archaeological or Other Literary Evidence for an Early Christian Presence in Britain?

We earlier discussed the New Testament literature and commentary by early Church fathers, such as Clement, Irenaeus, Tertullian, Eusebius and others, that are explicit that Christianity had spread to Britain early on – and that Christ's original disciples or Apostles were involved. Unfortunately, these early testimonies do not name the disciples. But by 1600, as we have discussed, even as high a Vatican official as the Curator of its Library – Cardinal Baronius – was recording that a ship or boat had sailed across the Mediterranean with Joseph of Arimathea and other Jewish refugees onboard. He also wrote that the ship dropped the passengers off on the coast of southern France, near Marseilles; unfortunately, he failed to include the source of his information. We have discussed the numerous legends all over that region that a number of Jesus's disciples had landed there, including Mary Magdalene, Lazarus, Joseph, and several more disciples. Most of the legends have Magdalene and many of the others remaining in mainland Europe, but curiously none of them suggest Joseph stayed there – he is always said to have left on an overland route to Britain and, finally, Glastonbury. Legends cannot be verified or used as scholarly evidence to prove anything, but it is difficult to understand why – if the legends are indeed simply based on imaginary tales woven by the French – they would not 'keep' Joseph in France? After all, he was an intriguing and important character in the gospel story.

According to the *Cambridge History of Christianity*[LVI] (CHC), 'No clear archaeological or literary data exists (to show a Christian presence in Britain) until mid-fourth century except shadowy traditions about St Alban's martyrdom (the *Catholic Encyclopedia* calls Alban probably the first British martyr about 304).' In fact, archaeological evidence for the presence of early Christians or Jewish-Christians (such as Peter) *anywhere* is extremely rare. The CHC indicates that the earliest Spanish Christian inscriptions date from 354, there is little evidence in Palestine before 300, virtually nothing in Egypt before the fourth century, and even Antioch – where the word 'Christian' was first created – has no Christian inscriptions before 300[LVII]. So, lack of such evidence in Britain is hardly surprising. But the difference is lack of ancient documents for Britain. The CHC stresses that 'Literary evidence remains our principal vehicle for tracing the expansion of Christianity.'[LVIII] We lack such evidence for Joseph of Arimathea in Britain either because he never came there (as most academics insist) or because any early literary evidence of this was lost, yet to be discovered ... or destroyed.

Book and document burnings of non-canonical Christian literature began almost immediately after Constantine legalized the faith[LIX]. The possibility that documents pertaining to Joseph in Britain were among them is not negligible. For example, British historian Gildas wrote about the third-century Diocletian persecutions by the Romans that 'Churches were razed, scriptures burned, priests were killed so no trace of Christians remained'; the British historian Bede wrote, 'Churches were laid waste and burned ... for 10 years.'[LX]. The reaction of Jews to the new and growing Christian faith was almost as harsh; influential Rabbi Yose Ha-Gelili preached that all Jews should 'Burn the Gospels!'[LXI] We cannot be certain of the toll on Christian records of the Anglo-Saxon invasions or the ninth-century attacks by the Danes. The terrible Glastonbury Library fire in 1184 destroyed many precious records – including perhaps the alleged 'Origin of the British Church' by Elfan[LXII]. When Ralph FitzStephen began rebuilding Glastonbury Abbey after the fire, he 'swept away the charred remains of wattle-work (depriving posterity of a priceless relic)'[LXIII], if it indeed was from an early century.

Of course, Henry VIII's Dissolution of the Monasteries in 1539 probably burned or destroyed whatever was left of such records. Perhaps it should not be surprising that there is so little British literary evidence for early Christians there. Even Vatican records have suffered serious – and unknown – losses; in 1810, Napoleon 'relocated' the entire Vatican archives to Paris. When he was finally deposed, the sitting Pope wanted them back in Rome but had little money. So Christian papers were sold to merchants for use in wrapping meats and fish in Parisian markets![LXIV] There is no way to know what was lost forever from our earliest Christian records. Even the existing Vatican archives may hold many unknown documents; according to a recent Archives General Secretary (Luca Carboni), there are fifty miles of shelves in the archives, many unexplored.

In perhaps the best recent review about Glastonbury, Rahtz and Watts[LXV] wrote:

Much of what has been written is of dubious value ... myth and history are inextricably woven together ... William of Malmesbury's history (*De Antiquitate*, 1125) was manipulated in later centuries so it is difficult to be sure what is original ... although discovery of new documents is rare, it is by no means the case with archaeology, where what has been discovered to date is a small fraction of what still lies buried beneath the ground.

Finding artifacts, or even the remains of any possible first-century Jewish Christians that may have been at Glastonbury, would require some very challenging and deep excavations; in the late 900s, Dunstan had the graveyard covered twice with up to 12 feet of fresh earth because so many wanted burial there.[LXVI] Even beneath that any possible Jewish Christian disciple burials would be 6 feet or so farther below, consistent with traditional Jewish 'trench graves' discussed earlier.

Further Intriguing Hints that Someone from Jesus's Inner Circle Came to Britain

The Bible sets Passover at the full moon near the vernal equinox (Exodus 13:10). Since Jesus's resurrection occurred on or near Passover, a controversy eventually arose as to *when* Christians should observe this event – eventually called Easter. For the first Jewish Christians, like Peter, there was no controversy; Jesus's resurrection was celebrated according to the Jewish calendar[LXVII], the day of preparation for Passover (14 Nisan, known as the 'Quartodeciman Easter practice'). This meant the day might be celebrated on any day of the week, not just Sunday. But by AD 150 or so, Church fathers in Rome were advocating today's traditional Easter Sunday observance. Sunday obviously finally won out, but it is curious that – unlike virtually all of mainland Europe – British Christians had *always* observed the Jewish 14 Nisan observance[LXVIII] for the resurrection. Is this a strong hint that first-century Jewish Christians could have indeed brought the faith to Britain? Old Welsh records state that three Jewish missionaries brought the gospel there at the close of the first century.[LXIX] Could some have come even earlier?

Britain's early belief that Joseph had come to Glastonbury and founded the first Christian church outside of Judea did not go unchallenged by other nations. [LXX] The French, Spanish, and even the Scottish all argued again and again, trying to persuade the Vatican that *their* country was the site of the first 'planting of the Faith'.[LXXI] The arguments went on at church councils in Pisa (1409), Constance (1417), Sienna (1424), and a final battle in 1434 at Basle between Britain and Spain. At the 1424 Sienna council, British Bishop Richard Fleming 'upheld Joseph single-handed against' all three competing nations.[LXXII] The British won every round, even though most of the legends have Joseph arriving on the southern shore of France and embarking on a long overland trip to arrive in Britain. Although the alleged presence of Magdalene, Martha, Lazarus (who, according to some of the legends, became bishop of Marseilles[LXXIII]), and others at the landing in France – giving them time to preach about Jesus before Joseph had even arrived in Glastonbury – seems like a strong argument for France's primacy, it failed to defeat Britain's claims. It was not until the 'clerical error' theories of von Harnack and others centuries later that strong and persistent doubts were created among many academics and historians.

In summary, there is striking evidence that *someone* from Jesus's inner circle – or a later first- or early second-century disciple – went beyond mainland Europe and landed in Britain to spread the news of Jesus. Was it Joseph of Arimathea, or one of his descendants? Although many in academia are smugly certain Joseph never left Judea, an objective review of this chapter does not lead to such a definitive conclusion.

The weight of the evidence – although only documents and legends – suggesting that Joseph and others may have come to Britain remains impressive but not decisive. None of the legends or documents placing Joseph in Britain or Europe originates from Judea; those that have come down to us from there place him in the Holy Land all his life. No ancient record earlier than about 1200 has been found that puts Joseph in Britain. Yet legends such as these may be based on a real event, for which we still lack verification. Whether Joseph of Arimathea saw Britain remains one of those tantalising mysteries of early Christianity.

ENDNOTES

i Ashe, G., *King Arthur's Avalon: The Story of Glastonbury*, Dutton, New York, 1958, p.240

ii Jefferson, Thomas, letter to his nephew Peter Carr from Paris, 10 August 1787, in *Biography of Thomas Jefferson: Memoir Correspondence*, Vol. 2, edited by T.J. Randolph, 1830

iii Hone, William, *The Lost Books of the Bible* (reprint of his 1820 publication), Crown Publishers, USA, Bell 1979 edition, p.9

iv Spong, J.S., *Jesus for the Non-Religious*, HarperOne, New York NY, 2007, p.128

v Bahat, D., personal e-communication, 4 November 2009

vi Scavone, D., *Joseph of Arimathea, the Holy Grail and the Edessa Icon*, originally published in Arthuriana. 9, 4, Winter 1999; also in *Collegamento pro Sindone Internet*, October 2002, p.9

vii Crossan, J., *Jesus: A Revolutionary Biography*, HarperCollins San Francisco, 1994, p.127

viii Funk, R.W., *The Gospel of Jesus: According to the Jesus Seminar*, Polebridge Press, 1999

iv Lowder, J.J., *Historical Evidence and the Empty Tomb Story: A Reply to William Lane Craig*, Journal of Higher Criticism 8:2, Fall 2001, pp.251-5

x Hone, 1979, p.9

xi Ehrman, B., *Misquoting Jesus*, HarperCollins, New York NY, 2005, pp.46-59; Forged, HarperCollins, New York NY, 2011, pp.251-65

xii Freeman, D.N., 'Joseph of Arimathea', *Anchor Bible Dictionary*, Bantam Doubleday Dell Publishing Group, 1992, p.971

xiii *Gospel of Nicodemus* 9:12

xiv De Zulueta, F., 'Violation of Sepulture in Palestine at the Beginning of the Christian Era,' *Journal of Roman Studies Volume 22*, 1932, pp.184-97

xv Bond, H.K., *Caiaphas: Friend of Rome and Judge of Jesus?*, Westminster, John Knox Press, Loisville Kentucky, 2004, p.20

xvi *The Burial of Jesus*, a free e-book available from Biblical Archaeology Review, 2010

xvii Schonfield, H.J., *The Passover Plot*, Bantam Book, 1967, New York, NY, p.158

xviii Stuart, A.M., *The Three Mary's, Banner of Truth Trust*, 1984

xix Tabor, James D., *The Jesus Dynasty,* Simon & Schuster, New York, NY, 2006, p.235

xx Katz, S.T. (ed.), *Women in Jewish Life and Law, in The Cambridge History of Judaism* Vol. 4, Cambridge Press, 2006, p.631

xxi Scavone, D. 1999, Endnote 37

xxii Cardinal Baronius (1600)

xxiii Lewis, L.S., *St Joseph of Arimathea at Glastonbury*, Cambridge, Lutterworth Press, 2004, p.91

xxiv Todhunter, A., *In the Footsteps of the Apostles, National Geographic* magazine, March 2012, pp.41-65

xxv Ehrman. B., *Jesus Interrupted*, HarperOne, New York NY, 2009, p.102

xxvi *Ibid.*, p.81

xxvii *Ibid.*, p.81

xxviii Blomberg, C., *The Historical Reliability of John's Gospel*, Apollos, 2001, p.91

xxix Lewis, L.S. (2004), pp.13-127

xxx Taylor, J.W., *The Coming of the Saints*, Covenant Publishing Co., London, 1969, p.177

xxxi Lewis, L.S. (2004), p.92

xxxii Poulain, Pierre-Marie (Head, Remote Sensing Group, National Oceanographic Institute), *Question about Mediterranean Currents*, personal e-communication, 15 December 2009

xxxiii Rahtz, P. and Watts, L., *Glastonbury: Myth and Archaeology*, Tempus, 2003, pp.61-2, 91

xxxiv Pryor, F., Britain AD, Harper, London, 2004, p.159, 222

xxxv Mendels, D. (Hebrew University), *Why Paul Went West: The Difference Between the Jewish Diasporas, Biblical Archaeology Review*, Jan/Feb 2011 (also personal e-communication, 26 December 2010)

xxxvi Gough, A., *Is England's Land's End Actually Just the Beginning?, Atlantis Rising*, Number 86, March/April 2011, p.33, 62

xxxvii Taylor, J.W., 1969, pp.144-7

xxxviii *Ibid.*

xxxix Ashe, G., *King Arthur's Avalon: The Story of Glastonbury*, HarperCollins, 1986, pp.64-5

xl Lewis, L.S., 2004, pp.112-3

xli *Ibid.*, p.129

xlii Clark, T. & T., *Short History of Christian Missions from Abraham and Paul to Carey, Livingstone, and Duff*, Edinburgh, 1884, p.61

XLIII Lewis, L.S., 2004, p.85

XLIV *Ibid.*, p.85

XLV *Ibid.*, p.134-5

XLVI Clark, T. & T., 1884, p.60

XLVII Tabor, James D., 2006, p.234

XLVIII Nickell, J., *Relics of the Christ*, University Press of Kentucky, 2007, p.56

XLIX von Harnack, A., *'Der Brief des britischen Konigs Lucius an den Papst Eleutherus,'*
    Sitzungberichte der koniglich preussischen Akademie der Wissenschaften, pp.909-16

L Tacitus, *The Life and Death of Julius Agricola, First Century*, translation by
    A.J. Church and W.J. Brodribb, 1876, from Wikisource

LI Knight, D.J., *King Lucius of Britain*, Tempus, 2008, p.118-9

LII Scavone, D., *Edessan sources for the legend of the Holy Grail*, in Proceedings of
    the International on the International Workshop on the Scientific approach to the
    Acheiropoletos Images, ENEA Frascati, Italy, 4-10 May 2010

LIII Scavone, D., 1999, p.1

LIV *Ibid.*, p.242

LV de Boron (1990), p.59

LVI Mitchell, M.M., Young, F.M., and Bowie, K.S. (editors), *The Cambridge History
    of Christianity (CHC)*, Vol. 1, Trombley, F., 'Geographical spread of Christianity,'
    Cambridge University Press, 2006, p.307-8

LVII CHC (2006), Tilley, M.A., 'North Africa,' p.381; Meeks, W. A., 'Social and ecclesial life
    of the earliest Christians,' pp.150-1; Behr, J., 'Gaul,' p.366; Pearson, B. A., 'Egypt,' p.331;
    Trombley, F., 'Geographical spread of Christianity,' Cambridge University Press, 2006, p.312

LVIII CHC (2006), Trombley, F., p.305

LIX CHC (2006), Cameron, A., 'Constantine and the 'peace' of the church,' p.545

LX Butler, A. and Jones, K., *Butler's Lives of the Saints*, Burns and Oates, Great Britain,
    1997, p.142

LXI Davies, W.D., Finkelstein, L., and Katz, S.T., *Cambridge History of Judaism*,
    Cambridge University Press, 2006, p.278

LXII Lewis, L.S. (2004), p.36

LXIII Ashe, G. (1958), p.281

LXIV Ambrosini, M.L. with Wills, M., *The Secret Archives of the Vatican*, Barnes &
    Noble Books, USA, 1996, p.295

LXV Lewis, L.S. Rahtz, P. and Watts, L. (2003), p.9, 38-9, 51

LXVI Strong, S. (Glastonbury Abbey Education Officer), personal e-communication, Jan. 4,
    2010

LXVII *CHC* (2006), Trevett, C., 'Asia Minor and Archea,' p.403, 553

LXVIII *CHC* (2006), Vincent, M., 'Rome,' p. 403; Edwards, M., 'The First Council of Nicea,'
    p.553

LXIX Taylor, J.W. (1969), p.157

LXX Ashe, G. (1958), p.301

LXXI *Ibid.*

LXXII *Ibid.*

LXXIII Taylor, J.W. (1969), p.107

'THE HALLOWS'

From my name has come a dream
A fable
A myth
A truth that runs deep beneath the daily round.

The cup of transformation.
The stone that falls from heaven.
The double-edged sword that extracts a heavy price.
The lance of perception that wounds and heals
By the Dolorous Blow
The sword of David in the Ship of Solomon
That sails out.

Timeless symbols resonate
Of Cup and Sword
Dish and Lance
They colour the essence of truth
That we seek what we cannot find.
Desire what we cannot have
Fear what we cannot face,
And yearn for a safe harbour of loving arms to hold us dear
Forever and ever.

Maddy Prior, from the CD 'Arthur the King'

'The Hallows'. (Courtesy of Ken Macfarlane)

BIBLIOGRAPHY

BOOKS

Barber, M., *The Trial of the Templars*. Cambridge, 2006

Ibid., *The New Knighthood*. Canto, 1995

Barber, R., *The Holy Grail*. Penguin, 2004

Carley, James P., *Glastonbury Abbey*. Gothic Image Publications, 1996

Currer-Briggs, N., *The Holy Grail and the Shroud of Christ*. ARA Publications, 1984

Dunning, R., *Somerset Monasteries*. Tempus, 2001

Escott, T.H.S., *Somerset: Historical, Descriptive, Biographical*. Mates County Series, 1908

Evans, S. (trans.), *The High History of the Holy Grail*. James Clarke and Co., 2005

Faith, J., *The Knights Templar in Somerset*. The History Press, 2009

Fortune, D., *Glastonbury Avalon of the Heart*. Weiser, 2000

Frale, B., *The Templars, The Secret History Revealed*. Maverick House, 2009

Ibid., *The Templars and the Shroud of Christ*. Maverick House, 2011

Lord, E., *The Knights Templar in Britain*. Pearson, 2004

McHattie, G. (Ed.), *The Knights Templar: Influences from the Past and Impulses for the Future*. Temple Lodge, 2011

Morgan, R., *Shroud Guide*. The Runciman Press, 1983

Pagels, E., *The Gnostic Gospels*. Phoenix, 2006

Rahtz, P. and Watts, W., *Glastonbury: Myth & Archaeology*. The History Press, 1999

Wilson, I., *The Shroud: The 2000-Year-Old Mystery Solved*. Bantam Press, 2010

Ibid., *Holy Faces, Secret Places*. Corgi, 1992

PAPERS AND JOURNALS

Agee, D., *Joseph of Arimathea* (Looe Old Cornwall Society, December 2006)

Agee, D., *The Celtic Origins and Pre-Conquest History of Lamanna* AD 500-1066, (Looe Old Cornwall Society, July 2006)

Carley, James, *A Fragment of Perlesvaus at Wells Cathedral Library* (The Chained Library, Wells Cathedral)

The Downside Review, no. 424 (Downside Abbey, July 2003)

Dymock-Herdsman, A., *Abbas and Templecombe* Parts 1-4 (1988/9)

Moon, P., *The Cross, the Resurrection and the Shroud of Turin* (Templar Print and Design)

Morgan, Rex. (Ed.), *Shroud News*, Issue no.42. (August 1987)

Morgan, Rex. (Ed.), *Shroud News*, Issue no.118. (December 2001)

Morgan, Rex (Ed.), *Shroud News*, Issue no.100. (August 1978)

Morgan, Rex. (Ed.), *Shroud News*, Issue no.113. (April 1999)

Riall, N., *Hampshire Papers – Henry of Blois, Bishop of Winchester A Patron of the Twelfth-Century Renaissance.* (Hampshire County Council, August 1994)

ARCHAEOLOGICAL REPORTS

Croft Andrew, C.K., *Excavations at the Chapels of Lammana – Draft Report. 27 January 1936* (Looe Old Cornwall Society File)

Nitowski, Dr E. *Analysis of Samples taken from Templecombe Panel Painting* (1995)

Time Team Excavations at Looe Island, Cornwall. Wessex Archaeology (2009)

Time Team dig at Templecombe Somerset. Wessex Archaeology (1996)

PRIMARY SOURCES

Notes by Rex Morgan – Lecture to British Society of the Turin Shroud – Templecombe Panel Painting, by Anna Hulbert (1988)

The Great Chartulary of Glastonbury, A. Watkin (ed.) (Somerset Record Society, 194-56)

If you enjoyed this book, you may also be interested in …

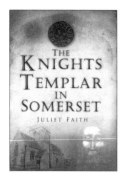

The Knights Templar in Somerset

JULIET FAITH

This book explores what life was like during the Templars' stay in Somerset durin
the thirteenth and fourteenth centuries. It reveals the struggles over land ownersh
in the county, and introduces the reader to little known historical characters
including William de Marisco, revealing his struggle with the Templars, and claim
the throne of England. Richly illustrated and compiled using original research, th
book is sure to appeal to everyone interested in medieval history.

978 0 7524 5256 2

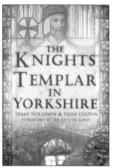

The Knights Templar in Yorkshire

DIANE HOLLOWAY & TRISH COLTON

Where can you see an effigy of a Templar? What prompted King John to hand
England over to an Italian? Who worked for the Templars in Yorkshire? *The Knigy
Templar in Yorkshire* answers all these questions and many more. This fascinating
volume takes the reader on an intimate tour of the ten major Templar sites
established in Yorkshire, and reveals what life was like for their inhabitants, how t
land was farmed, what the population ate, how they were taxed and local legend

978 0 7509 5087 9

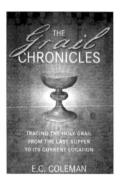

The Grail Chronicles

E.C. COLEMAN

This is the story of a plain silver chalice from the first century AD that now rests in t
heart of England. From its momentous beginnings as the cup used by Christ at the
Supper, and as the vessel used to catch His blood at the Crucifixion, to its unrecogn
discovery in the late nineteenth century, the chalice has passed through the hands o
saints, crusaders, kings, queens, Templar knights and 'Guardians'. This account revisit
beginnings of the Knights Templar and their rise to incredible wealth and power; b
most importantly of all, however, it establishes where the Holy Grail is now.

978 0 7524 5532 7

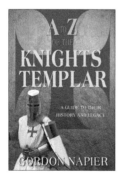

A-Z of the Knights Templar

GORDON NAPIER

The Knights Templar was the foremost Military Order of the Crusades. In abou
1118 these warrior-monks were appointed custodians of Temple Mount, and
defenders of Christian pilgrims in the Holy Land. Endorsed by the Catholic
Church in 1129, the Order became a favoured cause across Europe. This highly
readable and informative A-Z guide is an invaluable reference to the places, peo
and themes of the Crusades, the Knights Templars and their legacy.

978 1 8622 7386 3

Visit our website and discover thousands of other History Press books.
www.thehistorypress.co.uk

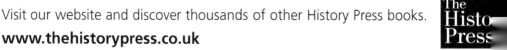